ISBN: 978-1-7325006-0-0

Dad at 17 in 1942. Medical school was five years away.

For Henway and Ski

TABLE OF CONTENTS

Introducing Dad (In His Own Words)

I always wanted to be a doctor.

It all began when my father, who would never take a day off, came home one day because of illness. I remember the doctor coming to our home, and though my father was better in a couple of days, he remained weak and dispirited. When ordered to take a week of rest, he chose a small Jewish camp settlement in Michigan where he rested, tanned, and became healthier. He returned to work.

At their butcher shop in 1941 — Sarah and Abrom Kamenetzky, Dad's parents.

I was then six or seven, old enough to be awed by what I thought to be a miracle; a miracle, not directly from God, but from a human who bore the name *doctor*. Thereafter, I was determined to become this healer.

Only a doctor. My father, a Kosher meat butcher, assumed I would take over on his retirement. I never gave that serious consideration. My only interest lay in always doing what doctors do: Perform miracles.

My father taught me the butcher's trade. He owned a small kosher butcher shop on the west side of Chicago from the time he arrived in America from

Dad with his sister Faye,
about 1930.

Europe in the mid-1920s. Even though I helped out in his shop throughout my childhood—wrapping purchases, collecting the monies, and going to the stockyards and poultry markets before going to school—I never entertained the idea of being a butcher as my life's work.

I had a Jewish upbringing. It was in the depths of the depression, and like most of our acquaintances, we were in the lower economic class. I never realized that I was poor because everyone else was in similar straits. I attended an Orthodox Jewish seminary three days a week right after secular school, and could have easily received an exemption for duty in the service by claiming to be a rabbinical student. Instead, when the dean of the seminary asked the boys in my class if they were planning to become rabbis, everyone answered "yes"—except for me. My goal was always to become a doctor, and I was not comfortable being dishonest about it. The other students received military exemptions. I decided to enlist in the Navy, with World War II

8

having begun some weeks before. (Using the word "enlisted" here is perhaps a misnomer, because I would have been drafted into the Army if I had not enlisted.) I chose the Navy after speaking to a Navy recruiter, who assured me that I would go to a Hospital Corps school where I would learn at least some basics of medicine. There was also a 1-3% chance that I could qualify to go to medical school. This did not happen.

Dad in the U.S. Navy,
about 1944

Soon after starting basic training at the Great Lakes Naval Station, north of Chicago, all recruits underwent a battery of written tests. I was subsequently chosen to take the final written examination called the *Eddy* test. (I didn't know it at the time, but soon learned that those who passed the *Eddy* test were put into a separate group to become radar technicians.)

After five weeks of Basic Training, I received my orders, taken to a train station and was on my way to my next assignment—which I assumed was the Hospital Corps school in Virginia. I took a seat next to a recruit I knew from training. He heard that I was on my way to radar technician school. "Wrong!" I told him. "I am going to Hospital Corps School!" He told me to look more closely at my orders. I opened the envelope I was carrying and sure enough, it said I was on my way to begin the radar repair training. I went immediately to the officer in charge of the train. I saluted him, and told him there was a mistake. I explained that I was promised that I was to go to Hospital Corps School. His response was short. "Shut up and go back to your seat."

That was the extent of the discussion of the error that I felt the Navy had made. That was also when I discovered that anyone who passed the *Eddy* test was going to become a radar technician. I passed.

Dad's certification as a radar repair technician in the Navy.

The following 2 1/2 years in the Navy consisted of 8 months of intensive electronics training, after which we were given the choice of the type of ships on which we wished to serve. The options were posted on a wall of the barracks and we were instructed to write our names under the category we wanted. While in the training program, I met a fellow recruit that became a very close friend, Leon Schlesinger. When we went to the bulletin board, he wrote his name under "Battleship" and I wrote my name under "Barge." "Wait a minute," he said. "Don't you know that a barge doesn't even have an engine? It has to be towed from one place to another."

"Right," I said. "I know that and that's why I took the barge. Do you think that they are going to tow the barge where ships are shooting at each other? You could get killed!"

"But Jake, on the battleship you get steaks at every dinner and movies are changed every other night and there's more room to walk around."

"Leon, " I said. "The name of the game is survival—not steaks or movies. I'd rather be on a boring barge than on a battling battleship."

Leon thought for a moment and quickly erased his name from "Battleship" and put it under mine on the barge—"The APB 39— The Mercer."

Leon and I were scheduled to go to the San Diego Naval Repair Base and await the barge. It was quite a long time before the barge came from the east coast (where it was built) to the west coast where we were to board it. We first saw our barge after being in San Diego for a little over a year, and I went on it once. During the time we were awaiting the arrival of our barge, we were working technicians at the Naval Base.

Leon was able to rise in rank to become a Petty Officer, Second Class. Unfortunately, I was never able to proceed beyond Petty Officer Third Class because of my inability to pass the seamanship test—which consisted mainly of tying knots, and identifying planes flashed on a screen for a fraction of a second. I was outranked during my entire stay in San Diego. I had many sailors under my direction for the electronic repairs on small to medium-sized ships. At times, I'd be taken to a ship that was more than 5 miles from shore, which credited me with being overseas. I refused to accept this as overseas duty.

Of interest was the occasional arrival of a torpedo boat for repair of their sonar or radar equipment that required special services. Whenever they would dock, I was assigned by the crew to bring a gallon of pineapple juice aboard. The seamen would empty the fuel of the torpedoes into a large jug. The fuel consisted of 100% ethyl alcohol. After they accumulated a gallon or so, they would take the pineapple juice that I brought (kindly donated by a bribed Naval cook) and mixed that with the alcohol. All the boats had a strict rule requiring the mixture to age before drinking. Aging was 90 minutes. The officers on board would look away during this process, but were always given the first cup of the "aged brew." Within a short time, the entire crew and myself were in a state of near unconsciousness. Luckily, so were the officers.

Dad in Navy uniform,
about 1944

We called that mixture "torpedo juice." The next morning, the officers would go to the supply depot to requisition more alcohol for replenishing the torpedo motors. Crews of the torpedo boats always looked forward to docking at San Diego. I'd give the cook $5, which took care of an entire month's supply of pineapple juice.

I was always happy with my decision to place my name under "barge." (As far as I know, the barge might still be there.) Yet, even while serving in the Navy, the idea of my becoming a hospital technician never left, and my desire to be in the medical field remained intact. During my stay at the Naval Base, I enrolled in five correspondence courses for which the Navy paid the bulk of the tuition. I took courses from various universities—the University of Pennsylvania and the University of Arkansas— were among them. The courses were fully accredited and all in the sciences.

The proctor for my final exams was a Chief Petty Officer on the Naval base. He didn't give a damn what I did. I could have looked up the answers if I wanted (but never did.) I was honorably discharged from the U.S. Navy in 1946, and I returned home to Chicago to start my journey to medical school.

How a Cockroach Got Me Into Medical School

Though my family was quite poor and could not afford the tuition for medical school, the G.I. Bill had been made into law and would eventually cover most of my educational fees. So I then applied to the University of Illinois and to Loyola University. By the time I had applied, the Freshman medical class for the next semester at Illinois was full. Surprisingly, Loyola University informed me that though I qualified for their program, they could not admit me since they already had their quota (10%) of Jews. That anti-semitism surprised me, having just returned from serving the Navy.

Prior to applying to the medical schools, I had enrolled in classes at Roosevelt University (then Roosevelt College) in Chicago. That's when the cockroach got involved with my medical school admission.

It was the day following the final examination in histology. Here's what happened:

There were four questions on the final exam—-each worth 25% of the grade. The grade of the final examination was the grade for the entire course. When the examination papers were distributed, I noticed one question that I thought was rather vague; to describe a myomere. (A myomere is the cellular building block of voluntary muscles.) Not mentioned was the species of animal myomere. I therefore raised the question as to the species requested. The professor's sarcastic reply was, "A cockroach," which I gladly accepted. (I had read the small print in his Histology book that described the myomere of an insect.)

It was apparent that the rest of the class instinctively knew the Professor meant a human or mammalian myomere. I was dumbstruck when, upon the return of the examination papers, I received a grade of 75—a "C." It was impossible to be accepted into medical school with a "C" in any of the sciences. I immediately filed an appeal with Dean Warren Courtelyou at Roosevelt College. During my hearing, I told the Dean what occurred.

"Professor Dropkin," asked the Dean. "Did you in fact tell Jake (the name by which I was known back then) to describe the myomere of a cockroach?"

"Well, yes, but it was a wise-ass question so I gave him a wise-ass answer and he knew it."

"Did Jake describe the myomere of a cockroach accurately?"

"Yes, he did," was the Professor's response.

"Then he gets an "A" on the exam," said the Dean.

Later that morning, I went back to the Histology laboratory to gather my belongings. Professor Dropkin was there. "Well, what will you do now?" he asked. I said I was unsure; and then I told him how I was unable to get into medical school at Illinois and Loyola—though a career in medicine was really all I wanted. Then a surprising question from the Professor: "Would you want to go to Chicago Medical School? My uncle is the dean there and I could place a call to him." I was taken delighted. "Oh, yes!" I replied.

The medical school dean told his nephew that he should send me right over. I hurried out the door, repeatedly thanking Professor Dropkin, who several hours before had been my nemesis. I would learn that there was a waiting list for admission to Chicago Medical School, but following my interview at the medical school, the dean, Dr. John J. Sheinin, said he would put my name first on that waiting list. I thanked him and left disappointed, but by the time I returned home, Dr. Sheinin had already called to say that I was in—but that I needed to immediately bring $300 to register.

A flurry of phone calls and visits ensued asking family, friends, and neighbors to help me scrape together the payment, which at that time was a healthy sum. Several people gave what they could and soon, I arrived back at the school with my enrollment fee in hand. I was going to medical school! And all because of a cockroach.

_____

The next few years were busy ones. I entered medical school in 1947 (the same year I met Shirley), got married in 1948, all the while studying and moonlighting as a Chicago cab driver to supplement Shirley's income earned as a secretary at the Chicago Board of Jewish Education.

THE CHICAGO MEDICAL SCHOOL
CHICAGO ILLINOIS

JACK KAMEN

(Clockwise from top): Jack and Shirley Kamen's wedding day, June 20, 1948; Mom and Dad at his Medical School graduation, June, 1951D; iploma received in 1952 from Chicago Medical School following the completion of his internship.

Dad's Career as a Doctor (In his own words)

I graduated from Chicago Medical School (now the Rosalind Franklin School of Medicine and Science) in 1951 and entered my internship at Cook County Hospital in Chicago. Then it was time to get a job. A paying job. I took the last fifty cents Shirley and I had, hopped on an interstate bus and headed east to begin my job search. 50¢ was as far as my single fare would take me. My bus ticket got me to Indiana Harbor, a tough steel town, part of East Chicago, Indiana. I got off the bus, and looked up at the window across the street. There was a sign that said, DOCTOR'S OFFICE. I walked in and got my first job— at the Indiana Harbor Clinic.

The Indiana Harbor Clinic offices were housed in this building.

I worked as a general practitioner at the clinic along with four other doctors and a dentist. I tended to my hospitalized patients at nearby St. Catherine's Hospital. Then, in 1958, I began a residency in anesthesia at the University of Chicago hospital,

(Billings Hospital). In 1960, I obtained a one-year Fellowship in pulmonology in San Francisco at the University of California, studying under the renowned pulmonologist, Dr. Julius Comroe. To supplement my income, I moonlighted at Sequoia Hospital in Redwood City as an anesthesiologist.

St. Catherine's Hospital

Our family of six returned to Gary at the end of the fellowship, and I resumed my work at St. Catherine's in East Chicago, where there was little work for me in anesthesia. So, I applied to become an anesthesiologist at St. Mary Mercy Hospital in Gary, Indiana, but was told that they already had two Jewish doctors on their staff—and that was enough.

I obtained a position at nearby Methodist Hospital in Gary. After one year, a Sister from Mercy Hospital called me and offered me a job. I was told that the Administrator of the hospital had OK'd another Jewish doctor at the urging of Dr. Gerald Thomas, one of the two Jewish doctors on the staff who had also been on staff at Mt. Sinai Hospital when I was a student there. I told them that I

19

would only consider coming if all positions at the hospital were open to Jews, blacks, and other minorities. The hospital agreed, and I went to work at St. Mary Mercy Medical Center.

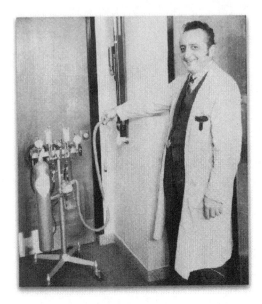

Dad at Mercy Hospital, about 1970

During my tenure there, I approached the administration of the hospital about opening an Intensive Care Unit (ICU). My training in anesthesia and pulmonology had given me experience in intensive care work, but in the early 1960s, no hospital in Indiana had an Intensive Care Unit. The president of the staff at Mercy was against the concept of an ICU, saying that every doctor took care of their own patients. But the next year, the hospital's executive committee decided they wanted to open an ICU. I became the director and spearheaded the opening of the four-bed unit in a large space on the hospital's first floor. Soon, the unit was enlarged to accommodate eight patients.

It wasn't long before we began to organize and host biannual seminars on Intensive Care Best Practices for physicians and nurses from the Midwest. Speakers in various specialties came to the convention center in Merrillville, Indiana (adjacent to Gary) to address the 300 or so attendees.

In the mid-1960s, I organized the hospital's first Coronary Care Unit, and became head of Respiratory Care. Soon thereafter, I established a pain clinic at Gary Mercy. When the hospital built a satellite facility in Hobart, Indiana, an additional pain clinic was opened there.

In a hotel in downtown Chicago in the late 1970s, a few hundred people gathered for a gala event to honor the Midwest region's "Catholic Doctor of the Year." Chicago's Cardinal Bernardin was there to take part in the festivities and to fete the honoree—which was me. A few short miles from the classroom where I had described the myomere of a cockroach, I became the first non-Catholic physician to become the "Catholic Doctor of the Year." A true honor.

Mom's (Shirley Kamen) pastel drawing of Dad holding his patented endotracheal tube.(See the **Manny Romula** story to read more about the tube.)

Mom was a juried fine artist.

A Reflection from Mom

(Written on March 31, 1971)

The life of a doctor's wife can sometimes be colored with unique events ranging in character from the ridiculous to the sublime.

During the 1950s when my husband was a new doctor engaged in the practice of general medicine, he was one of the dwindling number of doctors (now almost extinct) who was conscientious enough to make house calls. Our children were very small then, but on those occasions when grandma was staying at our house, I was free to accompany him on some of his night calls. On one particular night we made a house call which has remained indelibly and vividly imprinted in my memory.

It was on a wet and windy night in late autumn when he was urgently called to a home in an area which was rumored to be dangerous. We were new to the Calumet region at that time and totally unfamiliar with the neighborhood from which this call had come. I was reluctant to have my husband go there, but he was insistent. I decided to go with him.

Cruising the area, we found it to be heavily industrial, and much of the housing substandard. The tiny grocery stores on the side streets were dimly lit and closed for the night. With a flashlight beaming on house numbers, we found the correct address on a tall, ramshackle, wooden structure. The directions my husband had been given on the phone specified the rear third floor entrance. We locked the car doors and proceeded down a gravel passageway to the back and then up three flights of stairs —sans risers—which made the ascent seem a bit precarious. At the top there was a long porch with four apartment entrances where we found the name of the patient printed on one of the doors.

A few seconds after my husband knocked, we were ushered into a two-room apartment by a young man who was probably not more than 19 or 20 years old. The room we entered was a combination kitchen and living room, and was a startling contrast to the exterior, with brilliant color and bold floral prints. The place was immaculate. Standing by a bassinet in the center of the room was a teenage girl dressed in a full length floral robe. She looked grim, but smiled briefly when she saw my husband. The bassinet, which was resting on a bright, red rug, was meticulously draped with what appeared to be a wedding veil. Inside, sleeping on pink lace and embroidery, was a beautiful, round-faced, dark-haired baby girl of about one month. She had a fever and other symptoms of infection. The young parents explained the problems they had been having and nervously watched as my husband examined the child. The young mother clutched a rosary.

I looked around the room and saw a large, elaborately framed wedding picture of the couple and numerous other family pictures. The exposed shelf above the sink held neatly stacked dinner and glassware and and folded dish towels. A crucifix could be seen hanging above the bed in the next room.

After about 10 or 15 minutes, my husband informed them that the baby did not have to be hospitalized, but that she should be closely watched. He administered some medication and wrote out a prescription for more. Greatly relieved, the couple asked a number of questions about the baby's condition, then thanked my husband many times. The father walked us to the door as the mother gently lifted the baby into her arms and sat down in an easy chair to begin the long vigil.

We stepped out into the chilly, damp night, descended the three flights, walked back to the car, and left the neighborhood without misadventure. It was but the first of thousands of calls my husband was to make in that neighborhood.

The Stories You Are About to Read...

... are 100% true. The names have been changed because of all the legal stuff.

My Dad, Dr. Jack Kamen, was, during the 1950's and '60's a general practitioner in a raucous, rough, and ethnically mixed section of Indiana Harbor, Indiana. He then became an anesthesiologist and Director of an Intensive Care Unit at a Gary hospital system.

When I came of age and melded with guests at home and at functions, I was privy to his "this is what happened" stories. He was/is never embarrassed by their graphic content because "this is as it was," and patient privacy was always scrupulously protected. These, then, are the most "how-could-this-have-happened" snippets from his professional life, jointly written. They were entertaining to his listeners through the years, and we are quite sure they will be just as amusing to you.

Really now, we couldn't make this stuff up.—Joyce Kamen

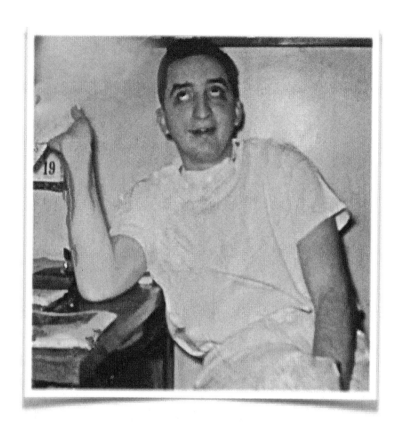

THELMA

Phone calls. One a.m. Three forty-five. Five in the morning. It didn't matter. They always came. Always another crisis. Someone's misery. Seemingly worse in the early morning.

It was two a.m. when this call came. I was out like a light, sleeping as deeply as I think it's possible for any human being to sleep. Coma would be the next phase. It was delicious unconsciousness. It was all I hungered for. But the phone was ringing, ringing, ringing...on and on and on...when would it stop?

"Do you want me to answer it?" Shirley asked. By this time, she was used to the nightly clamor of the telephone, but on this particular night, I was slow to rouse.

"No, that's alright, I'll get it." I said. I finally picked up the phone. "Yes, Kamen here."

The voice was a familiar one , but the speech was uncharacteristically slurred, almost unintelligible. He was unmistakably drunk...and horribly frightened.

"Jack, can you come over to my office now? Right now? Can you rush?"

"Who is this?" I asked, still puzzled.

"Jack, please!" he pleaded. "Come to my office right now! I really need you here now!"

"Who is this?!"

"Jack, this is Zolar."

"Zolar?"

"Yes, Dr. Bainkel."

28

So THAT was his first name. Zolar. I knew that he was Serbian, but everyone at the hospital just called him "Dr. Zee". I just never knew what it stood for. Zolar Bainkel was on the phone at two in the morning begging for my help.

"Jack, can you come?"

"What's wrong?"

"I can't explain it on the phone. Trust me, please!"

"Your office?"

"You know...on the corner of St. Louis Avenue and uh..uh..."

I waited on the other end of the phone."Oh God! Let's see now...uh...yeah. It's Deodar. It's St. Louis and Deodar. Please rush! Please!"

I hung up. I lay in bed somewhere between sleep and terror as the stark reality of the situation sunk in. It was two a.m. and bitterly cold. It was a thirty minute drive to the other side of town and who the hell knew what the problem was on the other end?

It was snowing. Ice and slush covered the streets. The going was slow. Thirty minutes turned into almost an hour. Would Dr. Zee still be there when I arrived? What—--what was the emergency? Very much a nightmare.

Finally (and with a small prayer of thanks), I pulled up to Zee's office. It was in one of those then new modern medical office buildings—stark, clean and shiny. Dr. Zee was an "older" doctor in general practice, probably in his mid-fifties, and adored (even "revered" or "exalted") by his patients, most of whom were also Serbian. "My life is in your hands, Dr. Zee," his patients would say. "You make me well." And Zee usually did by dispensing 80% platitudes and 20% medical services. He spoke their language. He knew their foibles, their ways. He was one of them.

I entered his office building for the first time that night. The office directory indicated Zee's office was on the third floor. I looked around the lobby. The elevator was not functioning. I started up the stairs.

I entered Zee's office without knocking. It was brightly lit by florescent fixtures that cast a harsh illumination over the office. Dr. Zee was seated on a chair next to a woman who was sobbing uncontrollably. Short deep sobs that came in sporadic gasps. He was rubbing her hand, trying to soothe and calm her. "It'll be alright...I promise...I promise. He'll do a good job. He's good. Real good. I promise...I promise..."

The woman turned and looked at me as I came into the room and suddenly straightened in her chair. She stopped crying and raised her arm. Her forefinger poked Zee's cheek.

"He did it! He did it! He did this to me! He did it!!!"

I knew this woman. It was Thelma. Just Thelma. Women in her profession rarely had surnames. She was just Thelma, the prostitute. (I was to meet her again the following year under different circumstances. That's another story.)

Dr. Zee looked dumbfounded. He was stammering and had a puzzled look on his face. His slow and unsteady movements were evidence that this night's revelry had included a great deal of alcohol. Clumsily, almost comically, Zee put his two forefingers to his lips. "Shhhh-Shhhhh-Shhhh-Hushhhh!!!!" But Thelma would not be silenced.

"He did this to me!!! He bit me!!!" she cried.

I had seen only the left side of her face when I walked into the office. As she rose from her chair and turned, her right side came into view.

"He did this!!! The asshole..."

Her right cheek and side of her neck were splattered with dried blood. There was also some fresh bleeding from the ear lobe...or rather...from where the lobe had once been attached to the ear. What had happened suddenly became quite clear. Zee had bitten off the ear lobe which remained attached only by a small bridge of skin. The dangling portion had already become mottled, and there were ragged tears on the edges.

"Did you try to repair this?" I asked Zolar Bainkel M.D., Zangres University, class of 1945.

"Yes, but she wouldn't hold still."

"Hold still? Hold still?" she exclaimed. " You're goddam drunk, you asshole, and you didn't even freeze it!"

"She wouldn't hold still." Zee looked bewildered.

I looked around the office. There were some unwashed instruments strewn on a stainless steel table, covered with dried blood. Thick silk, much too heavy for a delicate skin repair, was on the table and on the floor.

"Do you have any fine suture and needles?" I asked.

"This is all." Zee said.

"Well, I can't repair it here then. I'll take her over to the E.R. and fix it there."

"My God, no!!!" Zee pleaded. "They'll call the cops! They'll talk, talk, talk...it'll be all over the hospital. No, dammit, no!"

Zee started to cry. The tears fell freely on his cheeks still flushed red from the evening's bounty of alcohol. Sure, I pitied him as he sat there weeping—looking nothing like the strong, in-control "don't-worry-I'll-take-care-of everything" doctor that was his usual bearing. But what was I to do?

"Zee, be reasonable! You have nothing here. Nothing I can use!"

That didn't impress Zee. He sat there drunken and crying, and Thelma needed immediate attention. Suddenly, the situation became obvious.

"Come on...we'll all go to my office." I managed.

"Great idea, Doc." Thelma managed a smile. "It's right across from where I live."

I knew that. The whorehouse was kitty-corner from where I practiced. I put a dressing on the ear, and we all made our way to my car and office. Zee opted to have a seat in the waiting room while I treated her. He was sobering and didn't want to face her. I anesthetized the ear, washed the wound, trimmed all of the edges, and approximated the tissues with fine silk sutures.

The whole repair took about thirty minutes. When I was finished, Thelma looked at her heavily bandaged ear in the office mirror.

"Think it'll be OK, Doc?" she asked.

"I really don't know, but I have to say I doubt it'll look like it did." I pointed towards the lobe as she studied it in the mirror. "Look at this. The hanging part looks pretty dark...not much circulation going on in there. That could be tricky to heal..."

"Damn." She turned away from the mirror and headed towards the door. Zee had stopped crying and was sitting in the waiting room, holding his head in his hands. "Thelma," he began. "I never meant to..." His words trailed off.

"Yeah, sure," she said, still angry. "You're a lousy drunk. Do me a favor and forget where I am. You try to come by again and I'll make you some big trouble. Got it Doc?"

His eyes were still cast downward.

In silence, I brought her back to her place of residence, and Zee to his office. On arrival, Zee was completely sober.

"Thanks, Jack, thanks. I mean it. Anything I can do for you...anything."

"It's alright...really." I was too tired to talk. I left him in his office and made the slippery drive back home. It was 6 a.m. when I plopped back into bed. Shirley was awake.

"Anything interesting?" she asked.

"Yeah, pretty interesting. I'll tell you about it later."

Sleep came immediately.

EPILOGUE

Surprisingly, most of Thelma's bitten off lobe healed quite well. Only a "V" shaped notch remained. I couldn't help but think that it looked like an identifying mark that a farmer would use on a farm animal. But it had no impact at all on her business. In fact, things were never better.

"The 'Johns' think it's cute," Thelma told me some time later. She had even taken to wearing her hair tucked tightly behind the ear to give it better exposure.

"They think it's a kind of tattoo or something Doc." she said. "I tell them it stands for "very good."

I don't remember telling that to Zee.

BIG JOHN

My first guess was that he had been in a fight. He ran up the stairs in my office holding a blood-soaked handkerchief over his mouth. When he coughed, he was forced to withdraw the handkerchief, allowing a coarse spray of blood to explode into the air.

Fistfights were not uncommon. Occasionally there would be a knifing, and rarely, even a shooting. Many times however, an object that was immediately at hand, such as a bottle, would provide a suitable offensive weapon. These usually did a pretty good job of either thwarting an attack or producing substantial injury to one's antagonist.

I brought the patient immediately to the surgical area of the office, and sat him in the special steel chair I used when repairing lacerations or attending to other minor injuries. The nurse, "Auntie Jane," was methodical, precise and swift . She carefully washed his face and the outside of his mouth. There was no apparent external injury.

I asked him to open his mouth. He opened as widely as he could. His injury became apparent. The front third of his tongue was almost completely severed, being attached to the base by three or four narrow bridges of tissue. The bleeding was profuse. To prevent choking, he lowered his head and let the blood drip into a basin held by the nurse. I didn't ask him anything, for I knew that a reply would be impossible.

By this time, Auntie Jane had assembled the suction unit and switched it on "high." It took a bit of coercion to place the patient first in an upright position and then tilt the chair backwards so that it became more of a table. Auntie Jane was suctioning furiously, and what she couldn't catch in the suction, the patient was swallowing in rapid gulps.

I infiltrated the area with xylocaine and adrenalin, the latter causing the bleeding to slow. With the bleeding lessened, I was able to staunch the larger arterial pumpers through the use of cautery. This was difficult and trying because his tongue was sporadically moving. Although the areas I was working on were numb, the tongue, which is essentially a muscle, was not paralyzed and therefore was in constant spastic motion.

In a half-hour, the repair was finished...at least as well as could be done in an office. The bleeding had stopped and the tissues had been approximated. The tongue however, was immensely swollen, still preventing speech. He refused, and I did not insist on, hospitalization where a better repair could be done under general anesthesia.

I wasn't to learn the story behind his traumatic injury until ten days later, when he came in to have the two large silk mattress sutures removed. (These stitches are so named because they are used to join large masses of tissue and are of necessity quite thick.) I knew his name from his insurance card that he showed to us after our first meeting.

"Mr. Hunter..." I began. He interrupted.

"John...Big John."

How appropriate. He was well over 6 feet tall and all muscle. His face was kindly, and he spoke with a trace of an impediment.

"Well then John. How did this happen? Got hit in the mouth with your tongue between your teeth?"

"Unh-unh."

"Oh. Then you fell on your jaw some way?"

"Nope."

"OK. I give up."

Big John was reluctant to talk. "Don't matter."

"I know it doesn't, but I'm locking the door until you tell me."

Big John let loose with a laugh...a laugh that rumbled forth from his body.

"You won't believe it."

"Try me."

"I'm telling you, you won't believe me."

"I will...if you tell me I will."

"Well, okay Doc, it was like this. See, I've been married for fourteen years, come this April. Joannie is great...she's really a swell gal. Swell wife. We never argue...well, hardly ever argued anyway...until the day I came in here. That was on a Monday, remember?"

"Yep."

"Okay, so Sunday, like we always do, we went to church. That's what we do every Sunday...the Zion Baptist..over on Guthrie Street. You know where that is?"

"Yes." I really didn't.

"Pastor Collins spoke for two and a half hours!"

"Yes, so?"

"So did you hear me? Two and a half hours! *Hours!!* We were there a singing and a praying and listening to the Pastor talk and talk and talk...all together it was four and a half hours!"

"OK."

"So anyway Monday I came home from work and sat down on the sofa and then it came into my mind...like right now that I ain't gonna go to church no more. I'm gonna raise butter beans, mow the lawn, fix up the house, but I ain't gonna go to church no more. I told Joannie that."

"Go on."

"Well, you'd think I hit her with a two by four. Know what the first words out of her mouth were? You're a black heathen! Imagine! Because I ain't going to church no more, all the sudden I'm a heathen! Doc, I ain't no heathen. I love God. I even love Pastor Collins, but I ain't gonna let him spook me with another two and half hour talk!"

"And then?"

"These are the first really bad words we ever had. I stood up from the sofa. And she's a little thing, Joannie is...no more than five-two. I wouldn't hit her. If I did, I'd kill 'er. I bent over and started a jawin' at her the way she was a jawin' at me. We were face to face with each other, not an inch apart..not a half inch apart. We just kept going fiercer and fiercer, on and on and then she stuck out her tongue at me. Imagine! What would you have done?"

"Uh, I really don't know."

"Well, I did the same to her."

There was a long pause. He stopped, and seemed to be deciding whether to go on.

"A mistake, Doc. A big, big mistake."

Big John's head dropped. He studied his shoes. Then he began again.

"As soon as my tongue came out, she had it."

"Had it?"

"Yeah. By her teeth. She grabbed it and held on to it as fierce and as tight as a bulldog. Tighter even. I mean she shut her jaw tight.

"What did you do?"

"What did I do? What did I do?" He looked at me incredulously.

"What did I do? Doc, I couldn't do anything ! I couldn't tell her to let go because she had my tongue. I couldn't push her away because my tongue would go with her. So what did I do? What did I do? I danced around a little bit. I did a little jig until she decided I had had enough and then she let me loose."

The office was silent. I noticed Auntie Jane in a corner. She had heard everything. She quickly turned away when she caught my glance. She grabbed a tissue and began to clear her throat.

"Well Big John, how's everything with you and Joannie now?" I ventured.

Big John looked over towards Auntie Jane. She was red-faced and holding a tissue tightly over her mouth in stifled laughter. Then he looked at me, came forward and whispered: "Things is fine, Doc, fine."

"Glad to hear it."

"Yeah Doc, things is so fine, they're just about great."

"Wonderful."

"Oh yeah...and I went to church on Sunday."

"Yeah, John. I figured."

FRANK

Frank was a new patient. He walked into the examining room with his wife, Francisca, behind him. After perfunctory greetings, there was a short silence.

"So, tell me what's wrong," I began.

Frank gasped for an instance and then: "I don't know how to say this, but I have a bottle of Charles Antell in.."

Francisca interrupted. "Number nine."

"Pardon?"

"It's Charles Antell Number Nine."

This was a broadly advertised shampoo. On the radio, billboards, newspapers, magazines. Always *Number Nine*. I never heard of another number, always Number Nine.

"Go on."

"Well," Frank continued, "we were just done intercoursing, and...You know what I mean, Doc?"

"I have fairly good idea."

"Well, as I said, we had just finished intercoursing, so I decided to take a shower. I always do after I intercourse her."

"I douche, but later," Francisca broke in.

"Well, as I said, Doc, I went to shower but the shampoo bottle was empty."

Francisca again, "Charles Antell Number Nine."

"Yeah, it was empty. I asked Francy what I should do with it."

40

"Charles Antell Number Nine."

"I already know what it was." I said.

"Well," Frank continued. "You wouldn't believe."

"Believe what?"

"What she answered me. She told me to shove it up...Well, you know where, Doc. I don't know what she was mad about but maybe it was something I did when I intercoursed her."

Pause.

Frank was obviously proud of that word.

"And then what..?"

"Well, then I thought I'd just go along with her. Just to aggravate her, because I didn't do nothing."

"And then?"

"Well, and then I told her the bottle of Charles Antell..."

"Number Nine," Francine interrupted.

"Yeah. Whatever. I told her it wouldn't fit."

"Then..?"

"Well, she said it would, and I said it wouldn't and she said..."

"Please, go on."

"Then she went and got some goo, same goo as.."

"OK. Go on."

"Then she told me to lie on my belly. Then I thought I was dying."

"What happened?"

"Well Doc, she gooped up the bottle real good and then pushed it into my bunghole. Wow. The first part was skinny and went in easy but then the bottle just stuck there. But did she stop? Did she give up? I'll tell you...no! She pushed and pushed. I started screaming but that just made her push harder."

"And then?"

"Then I felt like a 'galoop.' The whole damn bottle of Charles Antell..."

"Number nine." I beat Francine.

"The whole bottle was in my ass."

"Then?"

"Then? Then she kept yelling 'I told you it would fit."

"Then?"

"Then we tried getting it out. You know, Doc, the bottle was glass and covered with (you'll excuse me), shit and goop and was goddam slippery."

"Then?"

"Then we come here."

I mulled over this catastrophe.

Finally, "Well, we'll have to get you a surgeon to open your belly and colon and take it..."

He didn't let me finish.

"Look, Doc. No-how, no-way, am I going in a hospital. No hospital. Ever. I'd like to die first."

"You easily may."

"I don't want to be a dumb-ass...."

Apropos.

"...But I'm not going."

My mind was numb. What to do? What to do?

A plan formed.

I called for Harriet, the clinic nurse.

"Harriet, we're doing an episiotomy on Mr. Newhart here.

"You're doing what?"

"An episiotomy. Same as having a baby."

An episiotomy, which is no longer done, is an incision of the vaginal opening that permits the infant's head to make its exit without tearing tissues. Skill is the substitute.

"You'll excuse me, but you really are nuts."

"I'll explain later, but now, get me a set-up the best you can. Oh, I'm going to use a lot of local, so get me a lot of Novocaine. Oh, and see if you can find an ovum forceps."

(An ovum forceps is a large clamp with very long arms used when removing an ovary. Miracle: She found one.)

It took about 45 minutes to assemble and sterilize the equipment.

Frank turned on his back and we placed his feet in the table stirrups and began.

We numbed the area and then cut the rectal muscles. With little skill and much luck, I was able to grab the bottle neck with the ovum forceps and work the bottle down and out. It was followed by a gush of pus and feces with an unimaginably putrid odor.

Frank returned in two weeks with a normal functioning rectum. All healed.

So ended the saga of Frank Newhart and Charles Antell (Number Nine.)

Humans have used body cavities to hide or smuggle possessions for millennia. Small diamonds would be secreted in ear canals. Narcotics would be transported into countries by human "mules" who would swallow cocaine or heroin filled condoms and eventually collect them at the other end of their alimentary system. Body cavities (e.g. vagina, rectum, mouth) are in current, common use, especially in prisons. A prisoner kissing a visitor may be effecting a drug transfer.

Frank and Francine's motive was of a more benign nature...sex play. Play in which Frank was the loser.

Sex probably explained the variety of objects, inserted in vaginas and then apparently forgotten which I recovered. Some were not surprising. Various dildos topped the list. But there was also a stuffed and sealed condom, a prankster's hand "buzzer", and a quite small empty perfume bottle.

The one of most interest was brought to my attention by the patient's husband. This patient had a pregnancy requiring special expertise. The couple decided that this care could best be obtained at Indiana University Hospital in Indianapolis. This required a longish trip from Indiana Harbor which prompted the pair to be in Indianapolis for two weeks prior to the delivery date.

All went as planned and the couple returned with a perfectly normal baby. The trouble began six weeks later when, for the first time since delivery, they had sexual intercourse. The husband complained of repeated sharp penile pain. On completion, he discovered small droplets of blood on the bottom of his penis.

That was when they arrived in my office for examination and explanation.

It did not take long to find the cause. A small sharp point of a suture needle was discovered near the episiotomy scar. It was easily removed. End of the couple's problem but the beginning of a problem for the university obstetrician.

When I called, he readily admitted he thought he was a needle short after the repair. He was less than elated that the husband found it, and I removed it.

There was a lawsuit in which the couple were awarded monetary damages. I do not know the amount, but I will wager that this was the first infant from Indiana Harbor born with college tuition already assured.

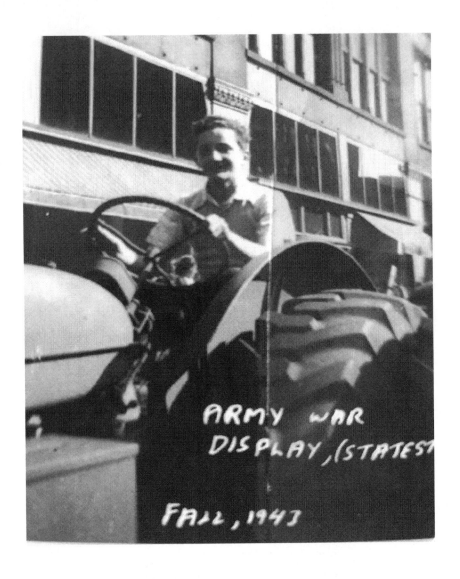

In 1943, Dad was about to enter the U.S. Navy. He was four years from the start of medical school.

WALTER STETSON II

Looking outside my office window that day, the gray and darkening skies mirrored my mood exactly...dreary and depressing. And now dusk was near— the day's smog was settling...casting a foreboding pall over the city streets and alleyways. I was exhausted and numbed from an endless day.

There had been a stream of patients. Most of them were members of the city's poor—restless, most smoking as they waited. There were the distraught, but not over anything in particular, just from the burden of bearing their daily great and small misfortunes and ills.

But the end was in sight now, and it was Friday. Delicious Friday! That meant a bowl of golden chicken soup that would accompany the Sabbath meal Shirley had waiting each Friday evening. (No better tranquilizer.) Ahhh. I could forget the smog, I could forget the bitter chill, and even the human misfortune that I had been working with all week— because I'd be home on Friday night, with a bowl of Shirley's chicken soup. I could envision it as I looked out my office window.

This reverie was not long lasting. There was shouting coming from the first floor entrance, my office being a second floor walk-up.

"Somebody help me up there! Help me! He's gonna bleed to death! Christ! He's bleeding all over! Help me!"

Only the receptionist and I were in the office, the nurse having left a 1/2 hour before. I ran down the stairs and in the entrance hallway was a well-dressed man leaning against a wall. His well-pressed and fashionable suit, shoes, hat, and tie told me that he didn't live in this neighborhood. His pants were down almost around his ankles and the front of his underwear was blood-soaked. It was apparent that the bleeding was still active as rivulets of blood continued streaming down his thigh. He appeared very weak and on the verge of fainting, being supported by both the stair railing and Thelma. Thelma was the busiest and best known prostitute in the area. She was was tightly holding a towel on his penis...which was the source of the profuse bleeding.

"Cheezis, Doc, I didn't mean it. I mean, I didn't think I cut it this deep. Honest to God Doc, I didn't mean it like this!" Thelma was pleading with me to forgive and to understand. This woman's career may have been at stake. Something like this could get around, and make her clients uneasy. And before you know it...well...she's a solo act.

Thelma's blouse front was blood-splattered. She was breathing heavily as she stood there. Her feet were halfway out of her five-inch heals, probably from frantically running in them while clutching this patron's bleeding penis. (Her place of business was just across the street.) Because of the lousy weather, there probably weren't too many people around to witness her arrival at my office. Good.

I don't know why I even asked, for it really wasn't necessary, but I felt I had to make some attempt at conversation as Thelma and I helped the bleeding man up the stairs.

"What happened?"

Thelma wasn't talking now, and the man was too much in shock to speak. He collapsed at the landing. I laid him down and ran into the storage area to get a cart. After much effort, we got him on the trolley, and wheeled him into the treatment room.

"I cut him, Doc." she blurted. "He wanted too much...too damned much. I do anything.You know that. (I didn't.) Anything! But over and over and over again...I can't do it! He didn't want anything

48

normal, you know. You know what I mean Doc. You know." (I didn't.)

I worked as rapidly as I could while Thelma talked. I gloved and grabbed a handful of hemostats (a scissors-like clamp). It was fairly simple to stop the arterial bleeding, because the spurting was coming from the main penile artery. The clamp was closed and the spurting stopped. The venous bleeding was more bothersome. The corpus cavernosi, or the penile bodies that become engorged during an erection, were sliced almost in two. These venous channels were completely cut.

I applied pressure on the severed ends for about 15 minutes. Because of their fragility, they couldn't be clamped. The venous sinuses were amorphous, shapeless. Finally, the applied pressure slowed the bleeding. Good clots were forming.

Thelma also relaxed a bit and continued her story. "He wanted to put it in every place except the right place. You know...you know." (I didn't.)

"First my ass. I let him, so alright...I let him. And then the bastard wanted my mouth. Can you imagine? The bastard! From my ass to my mouth! Can you imagine?" (I could.)

"Well, I said 'hell no'! I mean, why didn't he just think of doing it the other way? So then he started screaming, 'I need it, I need it.' Geez. He started moving me down and pushing me and pulling my head back and screaming and screaming, 'I need it, I need it!' Do you understand Doc?"

(I did.)

"Well, I fought with him and then got up off the bed and ran and got my straight razor that I use for my legs and for protection. Doc, I didn't mean to cut him that deep. I didn't mean it, I really didn't. I just wanted to scare him. To calm him down."

I started an intravenous infusion and a pint of artificial plasma and a liter of salt solution. His blood pressure rose, and his pulse which was racing but feeble, regained its strength and normal rhythm. I pulled out a blank chart.

"What's your name?" I asked.

"Do you really need it?"

"Legally and medical-legally I do."

"Are you going to call the police?" he added, retaining his anonymity.

"I have to."

Both he and Thelma gasped. They looked at each other, but they didn't have to speak. It was obvious that by now they were both united in pursuit of a single mission: To stop the Doc from letting the cops know that Thelma's kinky but well-dressed John had his penis carved because it wanted to visit places that weren't exactly open for business.

He: "Please Doc, don't! Don't! It'll ruin me..my family...everything...my job...my life!"

She: "I can't take another bust! It'll be a year! I can't do it!"

Their pleadings worked. Oh what the hell, I guess it wouldn't hurt not to call this once. "OK At least tell me your name."

"Walter Stetson." Pause. "The second."

"Occupation?"

"I'm Vice-President of Foreign Operations at Deppes Steel. Home base Pittsburgh."

That was my next question. "Here on business?"

"Yes. I was having a great day too—uh--until now. The son-of-a-bitch I met with today told me to call Thelma."

"You've got a problem, Walter. A big medical problem. The veins of your penis are cut. Both channels have been cut. Luckily, your urethra is intact, but you need a highly-skilled repair job. You've got to go to the hospital. I'll call a urologist and get him down here." (There was no urologist in our immediate area.)

"No way, Doc, no way. I'd rather die, and I mean that. I'd rather die than go to the hospital."

"Now wait Walter. If you don't want to go to the hospital here, then I'll get you in at one of the University of Chicago Hospitals."

"I guess you don't understand, Doc. I'm not going in...not here, not in Chicago, not anywhere. I mean it."

No one spoke. Walter, looking pathetic on the table, had an expression of utter hopelessness on his face. He seemed defeated, without any fight left in him. Regardless, I knew he meant what he said.

"You do the best you can here, Doc."

Damn. Now what was I supposed to do? The kind of surgery Walter needed should only be done by a skilled urologist. I could probably do a decent temporary job, enough to get him by until he got to the hospital...but I had never seen, heard of or studied this kind of repair. Do the best I can? We were about to find out what my best would be. I felt like someone who had to take control of an airborne plane without knowing how to fly.

"Walter, you should know that I've never done this kind of thing before."

"I don't care. Do what you can."

I began to assemble as many of the more delicate instruments as I could find. That this was even happening was unbelievable, but arguing with Walter was pointless. So was my doing this surgery.

By this time, the bleeding had decreased to a small, but still disturbing ooze. The tough layers surrounding the venous plexus were approximated. A plastic repair of skin (using the multiple ultra-thin sutures) would be more time consuming, but cosmetically, better results could be expected.

Two hours later, the job was done. "I hope it heals okay." I said.

"Not half as much as I do."

"Come back in 10 days and I'll take out the stitches."

Now he looked worried. "I'm going back to Pittsburgh. But I'm due back here in three weeks. Will that be OK.?"

"I guess so. But you can have them taken out by your family doctor in Pittsburgh."

"My family doctor? Doc, you're not crazy are you? I'll be here in three weeks. Will that be OK.?"

"I guess so." I said. "But what are you going to tell your wife?"

"Machinery. There's lots of dangerous machinery in the mill. I got it caught in a shear."

"Sounds okay. But what if she asks you what your penis was doing in a shear? And what if she asks you why it wasn't completely amputated?"

"No, don't worry about that. I'll rip my pants near the fly and tell her it got caught in some gears."

"Good luck."

"Yeah...thanks."

52

Thelma didn't utter a word during the entire repair. As Walter Stetson II gingerly got up from the table and began to dress, Thelma looked at me once again with her now sparkling eyes.

"Hey thanks Doc. Thanks a lot. You know Doc, all the girls think you're the best...really. You really take care of them."

"Medically... medically...I take care of them medically, Thelma."

"Yeah, medically, Doc." said Walter, smiling. Thelma giggled, nodded her thanks again and they left.

Walter Stetson II didn't return to the office for four weeks. Because my patients never had appointments, Walter just came in, put his name on the list, and waited with the others in the crowded waiting room.

"Well, Doctor, I think I've got a little trouble." said Walter nervously as I entered the examination room.

"Didn't it heal OK.?"

"Well yeah Doc..sure, it healed...but uh...uh...it has sixty degrees on it."

"Sixty degrees?"

"Well, actually, one twenty."

"One twenty?"

"Yeah. You see, it healed at an angle."

"At an angle?" I noticed that my tone of voice was becoming unintentionally strident.

"Yeah, well look here, Doc."

I watched as Walter Stetson II lowered his pants and shorts. Though the penis was flaccid, halfway in its descent, it angled upwards at, well, about sixty degrees.

"Well Walter, I see the sixty degrees you're talking about, but what do you mean one twenty?"

"Well, when it's erected, it doesn't all erect. Only the first half erects. The last half stays as limp as it is now, and you wouldn't believe it, but it falls downwards about sixty degrees. It's the damndest thing!"

I could agree with that. "Yes," I said, "Sixty down and sixty up...or maybe it's just the opposite. Yep...one-twenty."

Walter laid down on the cart and I began to remove the skin sutures that had not already fallen out.

"Uh...uh...uh...it...of course it doesn't work...does it?" It wasn't a necessary question.

"Works even better than before..according to the wife!"

"Well, of course. Uh...so what did your wife say?"

"She wanted to call the plant and talk to the safety engineer. She's going to write to our congressman. She's on a crusade now for more safety in the workplace."

Well, I thought, that's a reasonable response. One minute she kisses her husband good-bye, wishes him a good trip, and says she'll see him when he gets home. But the next thing she knows, a hungry shear in search of prey in a steel plant goes whacky, zeroes in, and decides the contents of Walter's fly would make a delightful lunch. Heck, I bet she even phoned Ike on the red phone about that one.

It would be one year before I saw him again and then it was purely by accident. I was making a house call at a small home that abutted the mill, when someone tapped me on the elbow as I was getting out of my car.

"Doctor, can I talk to you for a minute?" It was Walter Stetson...The Second. "I think you should know, about three months after I last saw you, the last half started to fill. Do you know what I mean, Doc?"

"Sure."

"Now it all fills, Doc! It's great! Just great! It still has the angle to it, but my wife says it's great! Just great! She doesn't want me to have it fixed. Isn't that wonderful?"

"Wonderful."

So Walter was off the hook. And his wife was in ecstasy. Thelma's straight edge and my surgical inexperience had made Walter's wife almost unable to wait for him to walk through the door each night. I don't think a steel plant shear could have done a better job. Oh...and, uh... you're welcome, Mrs. Walter Stetson. The Second.

*Dad with his Navy buddies
in 1944.*

MY-T-FINE

Suffice it to say that in my third year of medical school, we were hurting for money. Shirley and I, while not in the sinkhole of poverty, were near destitution. Though Shirley worked full time as a secretary at the Board of Jewish Education, we could barely meet the demands of daily living expenses. I owned one nylon shirt that Shirley washed for me each evening, and I wore it the next day. Shirley yearned to have at least two pairs of underpants. So when a job came along...ANY job...I took it.

During my years in med school, I drove a cab at night whenever I could. The job paid little, it cut into my study time, and when I think back, it was a dangerous thing to do...cruising the empty, darkened streets of Chicago, picking up drunken fares. Physical fatigue was a problem.

When the call came from a graduating senior, it was as though a major financial breakthrough had occurred.

"Jack, take call as an extern at Barker Hospital. Ten bucks a night. You'll sleep most of the time. You just do H&P's (Histories and Physicals) on surgery patients."

Could this be true? I was only in my third year of med school, so it would be a few months until I could "legally" take an externship, but I was being offered ten dollars! A week's rent! It was food! We would feel rich! What difference would a few months make anyway? Besides, the job sounded simple enough.

A week later, I arrived at Barker's for my first duty night. No sweat, I thought. Just stay cool. All I had to do was take a couple of H&P's, and then act as liaison between the patient, nurse, and attending doctor. The nurses there knew everything. A piece of cake.

After making rounds, I went into the Doctor's lounge and was asleep on the couch for about 45 minutes when the phone woke me.

"This is Nurse Sauer. We have a patient in the E.R. He says he won't talk to anyone but a male doctor or nurse. We have none of those here. You're the closest."

"OK. I'll be right down." This is going to be interesting. It would prove to be prophetic.

I got up and made my way down to Emergency. I went into the exam room and discovered a sheepish man, slightly built, standing erect, but with his head so low that his chin nearly touched his chest. His wife (girlfriend?) walked to the opposite side of the room, sat down, and lowered her head. They had a look of total defeat. He mumbled something that I couldn't understand. I asked him if he could repeat himself.

"Could we go somewhere real private?" he asked. He looked at Nurse Sauer. She turned and left the room. So only he, I, and the girl remained in the large examination room.

"Doc, I got a can stuck."

"A can of what stuck where?" I had no clue.

"It's a can of MY-T-FINE orange juice concentrate. It's empty. It's stuck on my dick."

Oh.

"A can of what stuck on WHAT?" After all, it was late, I had been sleeping, and I may not have heard exactly right. Besides, I didn't know what else to say. Having him repeat the problem again would buy me some more time until I had to respond again.

"Well, y'see, Jane..." His voice began to trail off. I shifted my weight to from foot to foot. He must have thought I was becoming impatient. At least subconsciously I was becoming very uneasy. He began again, this time speaking loudly.

"Well, y'see. Jane...she told me it would fit easy, but I said it wouldn't and she said 'Dammit it's not that big' ...so I opened the can on both ends...lousy can opener, you know, the rocking kind...leaves the metal jagged, and it fit, but not by much and then it got stuck."

"Got stuck?"

"Yeah, lousy can opener. The metal jags dug into my skin and I couldn't get it off."

"When did this happen?" I asked.

"Late last night."

"Late last night?" I had to get my thoughts in order. They didn't teach this in school. If they would have, what would they name the course? Penis in O.J. Can 101? I wonder what the lab section would be like? Did they teach this in urology? Psychiatry? Confusing.

"Late last night?" I asked.

"Yeah."

"What have you been doing since then?"

"I waited until Sears opened this morning."

"Sears?"

"Yeah, Sears. I bought a tool kit. You know, files, pliers, and tin snippers."

"Then I went home, but it hurt too damn much to work on it. It got all puffed and bleeding and it hurts so damn much that I can't stand it. And it burns."

"Doc," he pleaded, almost in tears. "Knock me out. I wanna die."

Jane spoke.

"It's all MY fault." She whispered. Then she lowered her head again and fell silent.

"I'll be right back." I said.

I looked stunned when I walked out of the examination room. Nurse Sauer followed me with her eyes as I walked towards her desk. She had a quizzical look.

"What's wrong with YOU?" she asked testily.

"Who's on surgical call?" I asked, not offering any further information.

"What's wrong with him anyhow? Bleeding hemmorhoids?"

"Unh-unh." Then silence.

"OK. Don't be a smart-ass with me." She was getting ticked. "What the hell's wrong with him?"

"It's an orange juice can."

"A—-a—-a—-can?" Good. I wasn't the only one that had trouble believing what this guy came in for.

"Yeah. MY-T-FINE concentrated orange juice. Small size."

"Where is it?" she asked.

"Where do you THINK it is?"

"His rectum?"

I shook my head. Close, but try again.

"No...it couldn't be!"

60

"But it is...stuck right there."

It was probably the image of this man's situation popping into her head that made Nurse Sauer jump out of her chair and head for the cubicle that served as the admitting office. She was laughing so loudly and hysterically that I thought Mr. O.J. MY-T-FINE over in the exam room would certainly hear her.

"Shush! Please control yourself! Calm Down! Stop it!" I was waving at her with my palms down signaling for her to sit and show some restraint. It was no use. She continued laughing. Harder now. Tears were streaming down her cheeks.

"How does it look?" she gasped.

"Oh for Crissake, I didn't even check!"

"You didn't look?"

"No."

"Well-l-l-l-l, Doctor, go do it so you can call Allegreti." she said. (Allegreti was the surgeon on call.)

Oh no! Allegreti! Dr. Luke Allegreti! My professor of surgery at Chicago Medical School! I'm not supposed to be working yet! Oh no!

I'd have to find a way to handle that, but first, I needed to have a look-see at Mr. O.J. MY-T-FINE. I'd think of something.

I opened the examination room door, quite sure that Jane and OJ had heard Nurse Sauer's raucous laughter.

"Uh, I'd like to examine you now." I said softly.

"Jane, will you wait outside?" said OJ.

"No. I wanna stay." Jane said firmly.

"Get the hell out..." OJ meant business. She left, her head still lowered, her feet shuffling as she opened the door and went out.

"OK. Take off your pants and lie down on the table."

"OK."

I could see the enormity of what was going on through his shorts. The MY-T-FINE can was pushing up against the slit in his shorts. The fly was pink-red and damp. Slowly... deliberately...gently...he pulled his shorts down and there...

It was awesome. The penis had swollen larger than its erected size. The can looked like a snug-fitting, very elongated naOKin ring. The tip of the penis was grotesque. It was bluish, exuding blood and serum. The bottom and top rims of the OJ can couldn't even be seen. They had become obscured by the swollen penis. There was a faint, fetid smell.

I covered the lower half of the body with a sheet and called for Jane to come back into the room to wait with OJ. Then I went to talk to Nurse Sauer at her cubicle, but I found she wasn't alone. Now the nursing supervisor was there, along with a guy from maintenance, and they were jabbering in a close circle around the desk.

"Get out of here!" I heard someone say.

"Small size?"

"I bet he went to the hardware department."

Then Nurse Sauer looked up and saw I was back.

"OK." she said. "Go on and get Allegreti on the phone." Then they all resumed their talking and laughing.

It was two-thirty a.m. and I had to call Dr. Allegreti. Maybe mentioning my name wouldn't be necessary after all. I picked up the phone and dialed. He answered on the first ring.

"Uh..Doctor Allegreti, this is the extern..." Oh God PLEASE don't ask me my name!

"From where?" came his quick reply.

"From Barker."

"Damn. Am I on call? Whaddaya want?"

"Well, I got a guy with an orange juice can..."

"You goddam called me to tell me you have a guy with an orange juice can?!" His anger literally jumped through the phone at me.

"No sir...you see, this guy...this patient...has an orange juice can stuck on his penis." My voice was quivering.

"Say it again...this time real slow." He was beginning to understand.

"It's a small can of orange juice concentrate. It's open at both ends, but it's filled with his penis right now."

"Don't get the hell smart with me. Are you from Chicago Medical School?" he demanded.

I didn't immediately answer.

"Are you a student at Chicago Medical School????" he shouted. I was doomed.

"Yessir." With that, my career as a doctor was over. Gone. Kaput. Someone hand me the keys to my cab. That was to be my destiny. Doomed to an eternity of picking up guys with weird things stuck on their penises.

"I know what you guys are doing. I don't give a shit, but this call better be legit or I'll goddam kick your ass out of school tomorrow."

Would someone please bless this man? Bless this fine, feisty, hot-headed Italian! Bless the school. Bless them all. I hung up and waited for Allegreti to arrive and take over the case of Mr. O.J. MY-T-FINE.

We could hear his nonstop staccato voice at least two minutes before his person appeared. The footsteps got louder and louder until at last he exploded into the examination room. He quickly determined who the patient was, and while I, Jane, Nurse Sauer, and the nursing supervisor watched, he swept off OJ's sheet.

His face pulsed in shock.

"Holy shit...what a fucking mess!"

"Gimme a pair of gloves! 7 1/2." As he gloved, he circled the table on which O.J. was laying. Then he went around again. Then from below, he slowly lifted the penis filled can.

An piercing scream filled the room and probably the hospital corridors. He let the can go. Another scream. O.J. and Allegreti were sweating.

"Fuck. We've got to knock you out and take you into the OR." Allegreti told O.J.

O.J. couldn't have agreed more.

"That's what I want! That's what I want. Do it now! Now!" He was pleading with anyone and everyone within earshot to end the nightmare for him.

The nurse anësthetist was called in. Nothing was explained to her about the case...just that "We need a general for a urology problem." Not enlightening her as to the nature of the case proved to be a bad idea. When she got to the O.R. and saw what was going on, she was virtually uncontrollable. Her guffaws and hysteria got Nurse Sauer going again, but finally, the surgical removal of the OJ can was about to begin.

With O.J. under, it was now possible for Allegreti to carefully ascertain the damage to the penis. Looking at Allegreti's puzzled face, it was clear he'd never seen anything like this before. Serious. The penis showed signs of early gangrene, and the odor coming from the area was noxious. Infection was surely going to be a problem.

Allegreti stood over O.J. on the table. Though Allegreti was scrubbed, gowned and gloved, he stood silent for awhile, trying to map out a surgical strategy for this novel problem.

Finally, he took the orthopaedic wire cutter. He managed to get one blade under the can, but that started such profuse bleeding, he had to withdraw. What now? What was he supposed to do now?

"Is maintenance on duty tonight?" he asked at last.

"Yes, Bud Carr is here," answered the super.

"Clean him up and get him in here now!"

"Bud??!!!!!" asked the super, unable to process the order Allegreti had just barked out.

"GET HIM UP HERE!!" The super heard right after all. Allegreti was about to make old Bud Carr a surgical consultant. Bud probably knew a lot about working with steel and metal and things like that...but when it's been wrapped around a penis...well, O.J...we'll get him up here.

Bud entered the OR and his face had a look of total bewilderment. He was wearing a white gown over green scrubs, a mask, a cap, and sterile gloves. He approached the table and looked at O.J.'s penis, grossly engorged, seeping, smelling, and wearing a MY-T-FINE coat of metal.

"Well?" said Allegreti.

"Is it sore?" asked Bud.

"Not now. He's asleep."

"Oh."

"Well?" came the impatient question again.

Bud's demeanor hadn't changed at all during his exchange with Allegretti. But as Bud looked intently at the unfortunate man's penis, he seemed determined to find a solution. This was clearly his big moment. He didn't want to flub it. Finally, Bud had an idea.

"Hacksaw the middle at an angle, so you don't hit the...the...the..." His voice trailed off.

"Pecker."

"Yeah, the pecker." Bud managed a faint smile, and relaxed a little now.

"And then use a small rattail file to get the rims."

Allegreti was silent at first. Then he nodded his head.

"OK, Do it." he said to Bud.

"ME do it?!" Bud asked, obviously quite sure he hadn't heard what he THOUGHT he had.

"Do it!" came Allegretti's hot reply. This time Bud knew there was no mistake about it.

"Doc, I mean...I mean...well you know...no license...and...well...you know."

66

"You're my hands. DO IT!"

What could Bud do except to do it? So he did it. I was impressed with the care Bud took; how gentle he was, and how skillfully he accomplished the "orange-juice-can-ectomy'". The procedure was about twenty minutes. Finally, Allegretti was able to get a cast spreader inside the cut Bud had made on the can. The penis was freed. Immediately, it began to swell tremendously right before us. (It wasn't a turgid swelling, but a water swelling.) The wounds were dressed. O.J. was then on his way to recovery.

When his mind cleared from the anesthesia, O.J. first looked down and made sure he was leaving the hospital only minus the can of orange juice and nothing else. That morning, he signed himself out, going against strong medical advice to the contrary.

No one was surprised when he left the glass of orange juice on his breakfast tray untouched.

EPILOGUE

I assume that O.J.'s penis healed OK He never came to Allegretti for follow-up and I never saw him again. Maybe it was because he started using MY-T-FINE in jumbo cans. Or maybe he's into the Pillsbury Doughboy's more pliable cardboard crescent roll cans. Now how did that jingle go? Oh yeah. "Nothin' says lovin' like something from the... "

Oh, you know the rest.

LITTLE TIMOTHY

As a general practitioner in the early fifties, there was a dictum that those of us in the profession had to live by. It was simply: *Keep up with what's new.* Splitting yourself into ten people and performing ten procedures at once would have been easier. The medical journals were proliferating rapidly. The constant stream of medical articles produced rivers, then lakes, and then oceans of data. Trying to stay abreast was impossible. "Reading" time was now "scanning" time. Because of the information overload, medical audio tapes were soon made available as a partial substitute, but this proved to be both a blessing and a curse. Certainly you could listen to the lectures while driving or doing something at home, but that left virtually no time for pure relaxation or even listening to music. *Keep up with what's new.* We all did our best.

While "scanning" one afternoon, I came across an article written in the Journal of the American Medical Association. (JAMA) It discussed the advantages of early circumcision, if indeed, it was the decision of the parents to have their newborn son circumcised. The article cited the results of a study on early circumcision which purportedly demonstrated that there was no increase in danger or bleeding problems if the infant underwent the surgery (yes, circumcision is surgery) AT BIRTH rather than 3 or 4 days later, or eight days if it was to be a Jewish ritual ceremony.

Great! This was going to be just great! It meant that I wouldn't have to make another trip to the hospital several days after birth. I wouldn't have to book time in the nursery's procedure room. And the parents would be spared the anxiety they usually felt in anticipation of the procedure. A small medical breakthrough!

Now all I had to do to implement the results of the study was to find the right pregnant mother and father...hope they have a boy...and have them sign a consent form for the circumcision to be done immediately after birth.

I immediately thought of Helen Giopolous. Yes, Helen would be perfect! She would be at term in about a week. I had delivered her other two children... two sons... both of whom she had circumcised. Perfect!

I called Helen and asked if she and her husband could come to the office so that I could explain the procedure to them. They came and listened intently, asking questions about exactly what would take place in the delivery room if their baby was a boy. At the end of the consultation, the parents agreed to have their baby son "done" at birth.

"And we'll name him Timothy. Little Timothy, Doc," said Helen.

Wonderful.

Six hours after Helen left my office, her labor pains began. Two hours later, she was in active labor, six days in advance of her due date. "Little Timothy" arrived at 1:38 a.m. Helen was beaming as she saw her son for the first time.

"Are you going to do it now?" she asked.

"Yes."

"OK, Dr. Kamen, but I don't want to be here. Can you bring him to my room when you're done?"

"Sure. It shouldn't be long." Wait that didn't sound right. "Uh, sorry, I shouldn't have said that. I didn't mean it the way it sounded."

"You better not! It should be long. The longer the better." Her face flushed as she again burst into laughter at the shock of what she'd said.

All this time, the delivery room nurse kept staring at me. Finally, after Helen was wheeled into her room, she spoke.

"What did she mean are you going to 'do it'? What's going on? It better not be anything crazy, Dr. Kamen. I'm not up to it. I'm just not."

"Don't worry. It's nothing crazy...I'm just going to circumcise the baby."

"Oh, OK I'll put you down for this Thursday at 4 p.m. I know your late hours start at 5."

"Uh, no," I said. "You don't quite understand. I'm going to circumcise the baby right now."

"What do you mean, 'right now'?" There was just a hint of panic.

"I mean now. At this time. At this moment. At the present time. Now." I said it jokingly, but she apparently failed to see the humor.

"Oh no you're not!!!!"

"What do you mean, 'Oh no I'm not'?"

"You're not doing it on *my* shift! Administration never approved this sort of thing!"

"Wait...wait a minute. Listen. Just listen. I—" She cut me off.

"No! I'm not listening! Why do you always come up with these nutty ideas? Well I've got news for you...I'm not doing it this time! Don't you remember when you put the baby's crib in the same room with the mother right after birth instead of in the nursery where that baby belonged? Don't you remember the hell I caught from Sister Bernet on that one? No sir! No way! I'm not doing it! "

"Are you finished now?" Silence. I continued. "Then perhaps maybe you'll listen for a minute. There's an article in this week's

70

JAMA. I swear that it says it's just as safe as doing it three or four days later...it's better for me and for the mother. I swear it! Let's try it just this once. If it doesn't work out, then that's it. Never again. I won't even ask. I swear. This can be a permanent thing though. Just look at how much time this will save all of the nurses! Just once...I swear. "

I got just what I was hoping for. After a long pause, mulling it over she said, "Okay, okay...just this once." But an "I'm not happy about it" look was on her face. I was in business.

"Once, just *once*." She had to get her last licks in.

"Just once, I swear."

As a general rule, newborn circumcisions didn't take much time. Using a special circumcision clamp, it was a pretty routine thing. First, the foreskin had to be freed, then pulled over a small metal bell, the hollow part of which covered the end (glans) of the penis. A metal ring was then slipped over the outer part of the bell, and the excess foreskin was pulled through this ring so that it caught between the bell and the ring. The ring itself was at the end of a bar, and when a large screw was tightened, the ring compressed the rim of foreskin against the bell. The foreskin was then cut off at the rim and after four or five minutes, the ring was released and the bell removed. The procedure, done this way, was almost bloodless because the compression clotted the artery and veins. Simple.

Everything went according to plan. Little Timothy screamed when the foreskin was freed and the clamp applied. This was to be expected.

Five minutes went by. Time to remove the clamp. First unscrew the ring...then separate it from the bell.

The large screw turned...and turned...and turned...and turned. It wouldn't stop turning and it wouldn't come off. I pulled on the screw and turned. No luck. I tried to tighten it again and then reverse it. It just kept turning without advancing. I started to sweat through my scrubs.

The nurse who had been assisting me now was glaring a deep 'Damn it Kamen, I told you so' kind of glare.

"What's *wro-o-o-ng* ?" She drew out that "*o*" like a knife at my throat.

"Uh, well, it appears that the screw is stripped."

"Whaddaya mean *str-r-r-ipped* ?" Her habit of stretching out those single syllable words was for emphasis.

"It means the treads of the screw can't catch the threads of the bolt. Must have been busted."

"Must have been *busted*? ?!!" She also apparently liked to raise the volume on two syllable words. "*If it's busted, you did it!*" You were the last one to use this set. This afternoon!"

Delivery room sterility aside, she stood straight and put her gloved hands on her hips.

"Now. What are you going to do *no-o-o-ow* ?" Gosh, I hated that.

"I don't know." I thought the honest approach best.

"Whaddaya mean 'you don't know'? Is this kid going to go through life with a whatsit on his widget? Do I go into his mother's room and say, 'Here, Mrs. Geopolous, here's your little Timothy. Oh, and don't mind that metal clamp on his penis. He'll grow into it.'"

I detected a faint hint of a smirk, but she quickly squelched it.

Wel-l-l-l-l ?" She was really getting steamed.

The next move was clearly mine. What was I going to do now? What? What? Little Timothy was shrieking, the clamp was holding on tightly, refusing to budge, and it was two o'clock in the morning. Hell.

"It was in the JAMA. I swear!" She didn't seem to care. Suddenly, I had an idea. "See if maintenance is here."

"*Are you totally out of your mind*? What is maintenance going to do?"

"He's going to get this thing off."

"How?"

"I don't know. That's why I'm calling him in for consultation."

She stood there, eyes wide open. "Don't take this the wrong way, *Da-a-achter* Kamen, but you're crazy. You're crazy and you're going to cost me my job! You're goddam crazy!!"

"Please call him..*STAT*!!!"

"I'll have to call the supervisor first," she said.

"Call whoever. But call maintenance and be sure you call him first! I'll be responsible."

"You're crazy! You're crazy! I know it's my job for sure! You are *GODDAM CRAZY*!" Her litany pertaining to the state of my mental health was unending and continued unabated like a holy mantra for the next several minutes. She seemed to take a breath only when she had to make a call or communicate with someone else going in or out of the room. Before long, it was just background noise.

The hospital had a rule: No voice paging after 9 p.m. In order to find the maintenance man on duty, (Bud Swalen was on that night), each nursing station had to be called one by one, then each department was called, and finally, security was contacted. It was security who found Bud at last, in the basement boiler room. They escorted him up to the delivery room.

Bud looked rather dazed. Only half awake. Nurse began to give him an overview of the problem. When she explained the difficulty with the metal clamp attached to the screaming baby's genitals, Bud became alert.

"*What th...*" Bud began. But the nurse interrupted him. She didn't want to answer much less listen to any of Bud's questions. She was far more interested in ending this episode. She took him by the arm and hurriedly ushered him into the Doctor's dressing room, and handed him some scrubs to put on. She also made a point of telling him to hurry.

When Bud emerged a few minutes later, he looked alert, but still bewildered. One nurse's aide pulled him into the room, and another supplied him with a cap and mask.

"Now keep your hands behind your back and don't touch anything. Just look. Just look." The nurse was clearly the one in charge here.

He entered the room, but didn't come all the way to where I stood with the screaming baby. Instead, he leaned far forward to get a look at the situation from a few feet away. For a moment, I thought he was going to topple over. I gingerly cradled Little Timothy, now crying with a piercing scream-cry in one hand, and the malfunctioning circumcision clamp in the other. Bud's eyes widened. I felt that this was probably the time to show him exactly what was wrong with the thing.

"Look here, Mr. Swalen." I placed the baby on the instrument table. "Look, this nut should screw right off, but it doesn't...see?"

No response.

"You see? It won't unscrew."

74

His eyes grew wider. He stared blankly. At last he spoke.

"Well, Doc, it's stripped."

"I concur with your diagnosis, Mr. Swalen. But what's the treatment?"

"Saw it off," he said. "I mean that...that...metal thing."

"Do you have a saw here?" I asked.

"Uh, look, Doc, let me explain something. If I try sawing it off the way it is here, I can really hurt this kid. There's nothing to steady it. You know...the metal."

"So?"

"So we've got to put it in a vise."

"A vise?"

"Doc, that's the only way. Believe me."

"Where's the vise?"

"In the boiler room!"

"OK, get it."

The nurse was now blubbering. "Oh my God! Oh my God! Kamen...Kamen...I knew you were crazy! I knew it! I knew it! My job! Oh my God!"

"Now just a minute." I spoke softly, trying to establish some calm. "This isn't as bad as it looks. We'll wrap the baby real well, and I'll hold him and you sterilize the saw and the vise and that'll be it!"

"Uh, Doc," said Bud. "You don't quite understand. The vise is welded to the table that's in the boiler room."

"That's OK. It doesn't have to be sterilized anyhow. It's not going to touch anything. Just the metal."

At that moment, Mrs. Flanagan, the nursing supervisor, came into the delivery room. Nurse Sutton was sobbing by this time and could only explain in short, staccato gasps what was happening. But now, Bud had become a different man. He was standing upright—at attention mode. Proud—helpful, taking overall control.

"Don't worry, Mrs. Flanagan," he said confidently. "I'll take care of everything."

Mrs. Flanagan put her hands on her hips and waited. She was a large and imposing woman. With any stress, her nostrils flared. They are at their maximal flare at this time. "I'm calling the administration."

Nurse Sutton immediately provided a a ten decibel wail.

"It's my job for sure, for sure! Oh, Mrs. Flanagan, I told him he was crazy! Honest I did! I didn't want any part of this whole thing! I told him he was crazy! He IS crazy! Honest!"

I thought that now would be the time to defend myself.

"Just one minute. There is absolutely no need to panic. None. I have full faith and confidence in Mr. Swalen's diagnostic acumen and remedial skills." (Oh, brother.)

Bud stood even taller now.

"Furthermore," I continued, "All of you can do anything you want, call anyone you want, report anyone you want. But I am taking the baby to the boiler room and allow our Mr. Swalen, to operate."

Mrs. Flanagan was apoplectic. She was only able to mutter her words, but then made herself clear.

"Miss Sutton is right," she blurted. "You *are* crazy, Dr. Kamen. You think you're funny, but you're not. You're not! You are *definitely* crazy!"

76

"I'll ignore that," I replied. "You're either coming or you're not. But we're going."

Mrs. Flanagan?" Bud asked. "Should I?"

She hesitated.

"Go on. You may as well. He's really got his behind in a sling." (She was a real professional, otherwise she would have employed a more explicit expletive.)

The march to the boiler room was mostly an orderly affair. We passed orderlies and nurses on duty at the various stations as we made our way to the basement. They could only stare in astonishment. We were by now a small army consisting of two RN's, myself, the screaming baby (with his metal appendage), and Bud; the latter smiling broadly and taking huge, confident strides. As we passed each station, Bud would answer their bewildered stares by saying, "I'm going to take care of everything. Don't worry."

The boiler room had a heavy smell of oil and was in a sharp contrast to the spotlessly clean delivery room. The place was unkempt. Dirty rags were everywhere and dust hung on the floors, the walls and the tables. It was hard to hear because of the noise of the water pumps and furnaces. Soon, all were shouting. Only the words, "He's crazy!" seemed not to need amplification.

We came to a long metal table where on one corner, was a large vise. It was a foot high, and had massive, menacing open serrated jaws.

"Just put that little thing in there, Doc. I'll tighten 'er up real good."

Now both nurses held the child. Like a large ship being gently nudged into the dock, the metal circumcision clamp, attached to the screaming baby, was maneuvered into the vise opening.

"OK., now hold it right there, everyone," said Bud. "Hold it still...real steady now."

Together, we became immobile. Slowly, Bud turned the vise screw. I watched as the vise teeth closed on the shining steel of the clamp. One more quarter turn, and Bud had it solidly held.

"Perfect," he said. "Now let me find a saw."

"What? You don't have a saw yet?" gasped Mrs. Flanagan.

"Hold on, everyone. It's around here somewhere."

Luck was on our side, because just a few feet away on another bench, a hacksaw!

"Should I start?" asked Bud as he positioned the saw.

"Please!" It was a chorus of three.

I looked at Bud. His face was stern and intent. Very carefully, he positioned the blade on the screw and slowly, slowly pushed and pulled...back and forth...back and forth. It a warm day, but it felt downright hot in the boiler room. We were all sweating, Bud profusely.

"This is real delicate, Doc. Real delicate. We don't want anything...you know..."

"I know."

In a few minutes, it was over. The screw was severed and the penis was free. Almost immediately, the baby's screaming became a whimper, and then the room noise again took over.

Bud was ready to offer more of his services.

"Everything alright Doc? Did I hurt anything? Can I do anything else?"

"Everything's great, Mr. Swalen. Just great!"
78

Mrs. Flanagan was next to speak.

"Bud, I really appreciate what you've done here. Sister Catherine (the hospital administrator) will be made aware of what you've done and how well you did it."

"Thank-you ma'am," Bud smiled, blushed and looked down. "Thanks."

The return parade upstairs was speedy. Mr. Swalen brought up the rear, and triumphantly greeted perplexed onlookers by announcing to everyone, "He's fine! He's fine! No problem! Everything's fine!" A soldier marching home in victory. A hero.

Not many people knew what was going on that night, but by the next morning, word of "Kamen's Circumcision Caper" spread rapidly through the hospital. People talked of almost nothing else for the next few weeks. It was topic one in the Doctor's lounges, in the nurse's meetings, in the administrative offices, and even in the boiler room. I'm told that it is still spoken of to this day.

And every once in awhile, I have to verify for someone that the story is absolutely true...all of it.

EPILOGUE

In spite of my actions on that fateful night, Nurse Sutton managed to keep her job and was promoted to Assistant OB Supervisor the following year.

Bud Swalen welded the remnants of the circumcision clamp to a small metal plate and mounted it on the wall of the boiler room.

Mrs. Flanagan laughed whenever we met.

Me? Well, I was not allowed to do any newborn circumcisions without specific approval of the administration.

Mrs. Geopolous had asked what had taken so long getting Little Timothy to her. I told her there were some minor mechanical difficulties and hastily left.

And Little Timothy? Last I heard he was the father of three children...all girls.

MANUEL

Cut throat competition between health care institutions is nothing new. Sure, we seem to be hearing more about it these days, but in Gary, Indiana, competition between the two city hospitals always seemed on the verge of coming to nastiness.

The Sisters of the Order Ancilla Domini (a.ka. The Poor Handmaidens of Jesus Christ) established the first hospital in the city in 1908. St. Mary Mercy was established for the people of the still struggling infant steel town. Up to that time, a private home was used as an eight-bed infirmary. However, in 1912, four years later, its monopoly ended with the establishment of a second hospital built by the Methodist Synod. People came to know Methodist Hospital as an institution not nearly as religious as Mercy, nor as dogmatic, and therefore, to many, it was not as threatening or forbidding. Before long, it became the preferred hospital for the non-Catholics, and for the newly arriving Jews. And, as Jewish doctors started to trickle into town, they joined the staff of Methodist rather than St. Mary Mercy.

Through the years, competition remained healthy. Both Methodist and Mercy strived to outdo the other by offering this or that advanced service. Both promised "TLC" (Tender Loving Care.)

Patients were often sent to the hospital chosen by their physician. This was dictated by their own doctor and rarely by the patient. Many patients brought in as an emergency were randomly taken to either hospital's emergency room. A busy ER meant more work, but financially, the hospital's money flowed out of the poor patient which was expensive but rarely paid in full.

It was in 1958 when 17-year-old Manuel Garzia arrived severely traumatized in the ER of St. Mary Mercy. Manuel had been walking to his after school job at the local "Priced- Right" supermarket when a speeding motorcycle came ripping through the alley he was crossing and struck him, smashing him into a tree. The cyclist was taken to Methodist Hospital where he tested positive for drugs and alcohol.

Two ambulances quickly arrived on the scene. At that time, ambulance calls were referred to funeral homes. The attendants were usually untrained employees of the respective funeral businesses. (Training and licensing of ambulance attendants was still five years away.) So one "meat wagon" took the cyclist to Methodist, and the other brought us Manuel. The hospitals were only six blocks apart.

We got the more seriously injured of the two. Manuel was conscious when his condition was evaluated. He managed incoherent speech. He had serious injuries, the most critical of which involved fractures of his left thigh and pelvis, and a ruptured spleen. His face had numerous fractures. Blood sprayed from his mouth when he spoke or coughed.

Most ominous of all were his chest injuries. Many of his ribs were broken on both sides. His lungs were severely contused. With each breath, his chest cage would cave inward instead of expanding, a condition known as "flail chest." Respiratory patterns were irregular and he couldn't breathe. His eyes were wide and he was staring...terror stricken.

We didn't have any equipment to determine his body's oxygen status— these were tests that were not yet common clinical practice. It wasn't needed—for Manuel was literally gasping for life.

Quickly, an endotracheal tube was inserted into his trachea and a bag was attached to it. Oxygen IV's were started and a surgeon skilled in trauma, Dr. John Dowlin, was recruited. Manuel was rushed into the OR (operating room.)

Dowlin was a new arrival to Mercy, having just come from a training stint at a hospital in Detroit. He was skilled in treating traumatic injuries.

Several IV's were started and large amounts of salts, plasma, and blood were infused. Dr. Dowlin rapidly opened the abdomen. He found the spleen to be ruptured. Its blood supply was then clamped and the spleen removed; and after other bleeding sources were repaired, his condition stabilized. Manuel's blood pressure slowly returned to a reasonable level and remained normal.

I attended to Manuel's breathing problems. His chest X-rays showed evidence of severe injury. The fractured ribs complicated his ability to breathe.

"John," I said to the surgeon, "He's going to need respiratory support."

"Very astute." Dowlin said through his surgical mask. He continued. "Now that you've made a brilliant diagnosis, do you have any remedial ideas?"

Do what you have to do.

"Well," I began, "I think he should have a tracheostomy. We'll keep him on a respirator." (A tracheostomy is an opening made in the front of the neck leading into the trachea, or windpipe. A curved tube is inserted into this opening and then attached to a respirator which breathes mechanically for the patient.)

Dowlin beautifully inserted the tracheostomy tube. After making sure that there was no further serious bleeding, Manuel was transferred to the Intensive Care Unit.

The next day, Manuel returned to surgery to have his jaw wired. A nurse attending to Manuel in the ICU had discovered that his teeth were out of alignment and that his jaw wobbled. Everyone else who had attended to Manuel and his myriad injuries had overlooked this. There were greater problems at the time.

On the third day of Manual's hospitalization, his mental status improved significantly. By the fifth day, he was complaining.

"I'm hungry." Those were the first words Manuel wrote on the Magic Marker Pad he had been given. He was unable to speak because of the tracheostomy. There were several devices we used to help voiceless patients signal their needs. One was picking letters or phrases from a large printed plastic placard. Another was simply hoping the nurses could lip read their mouthings. But writing on a pad of paper, or as in Manuel's case a children's magic marker pad, allowed communication. Manuel had no trouble making himself understood. He underlined the words 'I'm hungry' several times.

"Let me explain this to you again." Mrs. Dorothy Fairman was the head nurse on the unit. She never stood for any nonsense. She was Irish. A devout Catholic. Not exactly tactful. But she was kind. Kind but tough...very tough.

"Once more, Manuel. One: You can't eat because your jaws are wired shut. Two: You can't talk because this machine is breathing for you through a hole in your windpipe. Three: You've got a tube in your nose going into your stomach and we're pumping liquid soft food into the tube, and that's how you're getting your nourishment. ?Tiende"

Manuel looked up at Mrs. Fairman and smiled. It was the smile of total innocence and understanding. Then he slowly and methodically picked up the Magic Marker pad and stylus and drew a large circle around his already underscored words. "I'm hungry." He put the pen down hard on the bed and pursed his lips as if to say, "There. So now what are you going to do about it?"

Mrs. Fairman stood there for a moment, and then her eyes brightened. She had the answer.

"OK, look. I'll tell you what I'm going to do. I'll increase the feeding of the food through the tube if I can get the okay from your doctors. Whaddaya say?" She was determined to be his buddy.

Manuel nodded his assent and shrugged the shrug of resignation. Mrs. Fairman was feeling sorry for him now.

"Look," she started again. "This stuff you're getting is really healthy. It's like a malted milk only with vitamins and minerals and everything. Believe me, you're going to get well a helluva lot faster with this stuff than with anything else."

Manuel's look of resignation was gone. In its place was one of utter disgust. He glanced at the transparent tube coming from the pump and into his nose. He could hear the soft whir-r-r of the food pump, and he could even observe the progress of the tannish liquid moving along in a steady column. He looked at Mrs. Fairman.

Then he wretched.

Once begun, the retching appeared to be intractable. He lunged forward in spastic bursts every few seconds for four to five minutes. In desperation, Mrs. Fairman clamped the feeding tube shut and turned off the pump. His convulsive-like movements stopped almost instantly. He was covered with sweat, but he looked relieved. Then a smile...a heavenly smile...lit up his face. He reached for the magic pad.

"Call my mom and my sis," he scrawled on the page.

"You know it's not visiting hours." Mrs. Fairman was back to business.

He took the magic marker stylet and pressed it to the tablet with such force that the translucent sheet was torn. But he had circled his words.

I was paged to go to the ICU. I gave permission for his mother, who had been in the waiting lounge for five days since his admission, to come to his bedside. His sister was with her.

Manuel was ecstatic when he saw her. He motioned for her to come to him and started to mouth words in an exaggerated manner. She bent over and looked intently at her son's mouth. Soon, it became apparent that his mother was expert at reading Manuel's lips. He "spoke" to her only in Spanish. She knew no English. When Manuel finished "speaking," his mother turned to her daughter who then spoke to us, in English.

"He wants an enchilada in the pump."

I looked at her but didn't speak. Then she spoke again.

"He wants an enchilada in the pump."

I looked at her again, then at Fairman, then at Manuel. I thought it would be a good idea to verify the request.

"He wants an enchilada in the pump?"

"Yes. With a jalpeno pepper."

"Oh. Just one pepper?" I had to be sure I got the order right.

She looked at Manuel. His lips were moving again.

"Yes. He says one will be enough."

Mrs. Fairman stood there, mute. This was unusual for her. She appeared to be composed, but then suddenly, she blurted out:

"Now look," she said, "There's no way for him to taste anything! This thing is going right into his stomach!! Directly! Directly into his stomach!

Do you understand? His stomach can't tell what he's getting! We're already giving him exactly what he needs! Protein! Vitamins! Minerals! Carbohydrates! He's getting everything he needs. And we're not about to put that poison into him! And how is that whatchamicallit gonna get through that skinny tube anyway? How? Do you understand what I'm saying??!!"

His sister looked at her mother, then spoke to her in Spanish. Then they both looked at Manuel. His lips were moving again and his sister understood.

"He says he can't eat this slop. He wants an enchilada today and he wants tamales tomorrow."

It was now after 1:30 a.m., and we're standing in the ICU taking orders for Mexican food for a stomach tube. Did he want hot sauce and corn chips with that? Sour cream on the side? And how about a Margherita to wash it all down?

Manuel's ICU cubicle was brightly lit. There were five of us in there, and we were at an impasse. We stood there silently for three or four minutes. The hissing of the respirator and the ticks of the clock were the only sounds to be heard. Then it struck.

"Let's do it," I said.

Fairman's mouth dropped.

86

"Do WHAT?" she snapped.

"Why, give him the enchilada, of course!"

"Of course. Of course, Doctor Kamen."

"And just how do you think we're going to squeeze that thing through THIS?" She held the skinny tube in her fist.

"We'll Osterize it!"

It was easy to see that Mrs. Fairman was not amused. But TLC was the name of the game, and if that meant giving the "customer" a twelve pound turkey through a feeding tube, well then that's what we were going to do.

"I'm calling the Chief of Staff! I'm calling the Chief of Medicine! I'm calling the head of the ICU!"

"Now wait a minute, Mrs. Flanagan. You know I was just appointed the head of the ICU! I AM the Chief!"

"I don't care! I'm calling!"

"If you're going to call anyone, call the dietary department and have them bring the Osterizer in here."

"They're closed." She smiled as she sensed victory approaching.

"Then call security. I can find it if they open up the kitchen."

"You know, Dr. Kamen, they warned me you were nuts. And I stuck up for you! I told them no! They kept warning me. But did I listen? NO! But I should have. Boy, I should have! This can wait until morning. I'm not supposed to be on this shift now anyhow. Kuzinsky called off sick."

"Look, we're on a roll here." I said. "He's been very depressed, and now he's willing to cooperate. Let's try it. Why wait?"

I asked his mother if she could bring an enchilada. She beamed.

Manuel's mother and sister left. Mrs. Fairman had become calm. Besides, she would have something to talk about at tomorrow's at nurses' report. Would she ever! She had security unlock the kitchen and went down to find the Osterizer. She brought it to Manuel's bedside. In 30 minutes, the enchilada arrived. Not only the enchilada, but also a few tomatoes and a jar of assorted peppers. I plopped the enchilada into the machine.

His sister looked at him and then revised her brother's order.

"He wants two extra jalapenos, some hot sauce and a few tomato hunks."

"Anything else?" We were here to please.

She looked at Manuel.

"No. That will be all for now."

I put in the peppers and the tomatoes and turned on the blender. A reddish puree soon evolved. But there was a slight problem.

"It's too thick to go through the pump. What can I add to make it more liquid?"

I looked down at Manuel He looked puzzled...stumped. But then his face glowed. He mouthed something in Spanish to his sister. She translated for us again.

"Malt beer. He wants you to put in some beer."

"What the hell," I said. "Get it."

Twenty minutes later it was Miller time. I added the brew to the blender, then after it was thoroughly blended, I poured the entire mixture into the pump and turned it on. Manual was smiling—beaming—and then promptly fell asleep.

And so it went for the six weeks that Manuel spent with us. He had his ups and downs throughout the period. He experienced temporary renal failure. But each day, he'd order Mexican food. His menu varied from day to day, and the hospital dietitian gladly obliged. Doctor's orders.

Manuel grew steadily stronger. His lungs improved and he was slowly weaned off the respirator. He became the darling of the entire hospital. The respiratory therapists fawned over him. He wanted for nothing. Collectively we spent many, many hours at his bedside.

Then came that morning, the moment that the hospital personnel had looked forward to: The day his tracheostomy tube would be removed, allowing him to speak.

There were already seven or eight people around his bed when I arrived at 6:00 a.m. They seemed to be as excited as Manuel. All had spent many hours on his treatment. Most worked overtime with no extra money paid.

I came in, and cut the tapes that held the tube in place.

"This is it, Manuel," I said. "Are you eager to have this out?"

He nodded vigorously.

The tube came out easily. I placed a gauze dressing over the tracheal opening and secured it.

"Okay, Manuel," I said. "This is it. You can talk now Manuel. Talk now...try to talk."

The first words he spoke are still, many years later, echoing through the hospital. Every new ICU nurse, every new respiratory therapist, every new lab technician and every new doctor is told of his utterance. His words still ring in my ears:

"I want to be transferred to Methodist."

EPILOGUE

Every year, for the next five years after his discharge, Manuel would never fail to appear at my office door, bearing a gift to commemorate the anniversary of his hospital departure. He would come by on his lunch hour. The gift? Every year it was the same thing: A bottle of Tequila. I needed it.

MARY ELLEN

You would think she would have told me, for she had been my patient for years. She would come into my office for various illnesses, or she brought her children when they became ill. But she never said a word about this. Never a word. It was a total surprise. If she told me she was a Martian, the reaction would have been the same.

"Hello, Mrs. Dickinson." I said as she entered. She certainly didn't appear to be ill. She was in her early thirties, with short dark hair and a smile.

"OK," I continued. "What's wrong?"

She briefly hesitated.

"Well, it's kind of strange. It's really nothing serious, but I have to have something done about it now. And Doctor Kamen, I really hate to bother you about this but what happened yesterday really made me come here. I've got to do something!"

I waited. She began again.

"Well, you see, my right eye falls out of my head."

I'd been going on just three hours of sleep and was probably overtired and just thought she said that her right eye falls out of her head. I needed to concentrate.

"OK. Now, say it again. This time real slow."

"Like I said, Doctor Kamen, my right eye falls out of my head. It's nothing serious, but I've got to have it fixed."

I could do nothing but sit still and think carefully before responding. Then...of course!

"Mary Ellen," I said. "You'll forgive me, but I didn't know that you had a glass eye. Even looking at it right now it looks...well...natural. I'm sorry. I didn't know."

I glanced through her file chart.

"And I don't see anything about it in your history either. I just..."

"Uh...Doctor Kamen...I don't want to interrupt you, but I don't have a glass eye."

"Just a minute. You just told me your right eye falls out of your head. OK, so it's not glass. It's plastic."

"Uh..no, Doc. Not exactly. It's my natural eye. The one I was born with."

My thinking was momentarily in a state of confusion. Her words echoed in my mind. "It's my natural eye...it's not glass..it falls out of my head." I told myself: OK Her eye falls out of her head. It's not glass. It's not plastic. It's her God-given eye.

All right. There could be a couple of things going on here. For one, she could be psychotic. That had to be it. Probably stress. Everyone has stresses and the symptoms are sometimes manifested bizarrely. She just couldn't cope any longer, and she was imagining that her eye falls out of her head. This needed a gentle approach.

"Uh, Mary Ellen, look...I'm sure things have been a little hectic for you lately. Perhaps something happened at home or at work that has put a huge strain on you. But stress is normal, Mary Ellen, normal. This happens to all of us at some time or another...just in different ways. In your case, it happens to be affecting your perception of the position of your eye in your head. I'm sure that..."

Mary Ellen interrupted me.

"Doctor Kamen..."

"These things just get to us sometimes."

"Doctor Kamen!" Her voice was gaining strength.

"Yes, Mrs. Dickinson."

"You think I'm crazy, don't you?"

"Well, Mrs. Dickinson, "crazy" is certainly not an appropriate..."

"But you do, don't you?"

"No, of course not. But it's just that stress can sometimes..."

"OK. Before you go on, can I show you?"

"Can you show me WHAT?"

"Can I show you how my eye falls out of my head, Doc?"

"Now look, Mary Ellen. Such a thing can't occur. You're not blind in that eye. The eye is attached to your brain through the optic nerve, and that nerve just doesn't stretch. The eye muscles don't stretch. The artery and veins don't stretch. I'm telling you that such a thing just can't happen."

"Watch."

"Watch WHAT?"

I could see that she was getting upset with me. She stiffened.

"Watch this!"

She acted swiftly. She allowed no time for any further comments from me. And then I saw it. I saw it, but I didn't believe it. I saw it. Then suddenly, a wave of nausea passed through me.

I watched in silence as Mary Ellen lifted the top lid of her right eye with her left fingers. Then quickly, and obviously painlessly, she pushed the little finger of her left hand into the lower lid under the globe of the eye.

It popped out.

It popped out of the eye socket. Attached to a pinkish sheath, it lay limply on top of her right cheek.

I watched. My nausea worsened. Sure, I had seen worse in my years as a doctor. I'd seen decaying corpses, a thief with the top of his head blown off by a security guard's shotgun, and even fetid gangrenous limbs...but none of these ever made me ill. But Mrs. Dickinson's right eye resting there on the top of her cheek did, and it was about to make me retch.

"Put it back!" I was reeling.

"Are you convinced?"

"Yes! Please! Put that thing back in your head! Right now please!!!" I felt dizzy.

Mrs. Dickinson pulled the two lids of her eye apart and the eye ascended from her cheek and re-entered the socket.

She then blinked.

I gulped. I sat there for a moment.

"Uh...how long have you, uh...had this...uh...condition?" I was feeling a little better.

"Oh, a long time...at least ten or twelve years."

"Let's see. You're thirty-two now...so you've had this since you've been twenty?"

"Oh, I've had it since I was in my teens."

"And you never did anything about it?"

94

"No. It never really bothered me. And besides, it didn't pop out too often."

"Too often?"

"Yes, you know. Only once in a while. Usually, I'd poke it out myself. It was kind of fun, you know. Kind of weird."

I agreed.

"But after yesterday, I don't think it's fun anymore."

"Why, what happened yesterday?"

"Well, Doc, that's why I'm here. Because really, it doesn't bother me all that much."

I listened.

"I smoke Doc. You know that."

"And I've been trying to get you to stop."

The subject always irritated her when we discussed smoking. She was irritated now. But she continued.

"Well, yes. So anyway, our bridge club met at my house yesterday. We were all smoking. All of us. Playing and smoking."

"Yes..."

"Well, I inhaled wrong and I started to cough. And I mean cough. I couldn't stop. I coughed and coughed and then my eye fell out. Well, that ended the bridge game. Doc, you should have seen the looks, the screaming...all the panic. Everything was happening at once. And you should have seen Peggy. You know Peggy Middleton...she's your patient too."

"Yes, she is."

"Well, Peggy vomited and vomited and vomited. She even kept vomiting after I put my eye back in my head."

"I can understand that."

"They all wanted to call an ambulance and someone said , 'No! Just call the Police or the Fire Department!' Doc, it was just terrible."

"So they didn't know either? I mean about your eye."

"No, Doc. Of course not. I don't think it ever fell out in public before."

"Oh, I see."

"Yes."

"I see." Her voice seemed as though it was off in the distance.

"Doctor Kamen, can this be fixed?"

"Can it be fixed? I didn't even know this condition existed! I really don't...I really don't know. Uh...wait here. I'm going get in touch with a specialist. Wait here. I'll call him."

I took about fifteen minutes before I was able to make telephone contact with Dr. Henry Gordon. He was the only ENT (Eyes, Ears, Nose and Throat specialist) in town. He was a good practitioner and a real gentleman. It was easy to get along with Henry.

"Henry, I'd like for you to see a patient I have in my office here as soon as you can. And then call me."

"Is it an emergency?" he asked.

"Henry, I'm really not sure how to classify this. The patient's right eye falls out of her head."

"Yeah, I've seen that." said Dr. Gordon. "They just didn't implant the prosthesis correctly when they removed the..."
96

"No, Henry. It's not a prosthesis. It's not a glass eye. It's HER eye. Her natural eye."

"Now look Jack..."

"Yes Henry."

"Jack, if that's what she told you then she's pulling your leg. There is no way..."

"Henry?"

"Yes, Jack?"

"You wait right there in your office. I'm putting her in a cab and I'm sending her there. Now."

"Now look Jack..."

"Henry, just wait there. Just wait Henry."

I hung up the phone and sent Mrs. Mary Ellen Dickinson on her way to see Dr.Henry Gordon. I instructed her to show him how her eye falls out of her head the same way she had shown me. I was impatient for her to get there.

I returned to seeing my other patients, but I found it difficult to concentrate. Her eye fell out of her head. I know it did. I saw it. I remember it. And I really saw it. Suddenly, my secretary buzzed my in the examination room.

"Doctor Kamen, Doctor Gordon is on the line."

"OK, I'll take it."

"And he's laughing."

I picked up the receiver.

"Well, Henry?"

"I couldn't believe it. Damn Jack, I couldn't believe it!"

"You saw it?"

"Damn right I saw it. And you know, you won't believe this, but it made me queasy. I felt like vomiting."

"I know what you mean. But I don't understand, Henry, is why she can still see, or why she can still move her eye when the muscles are so stretched. Why?"

"Jack, look, I don't understand either. I don't understand any of this. Nothing. I'm sending her to my friend at the University of Chicago. I'll keep in touch."

Three weeks later, I ran into Henry in the hospital corridor. "I'm glad I ran into you, Jack. I've been carrying this letter with me from the U of C. It's about Mary Ellen Dickinson. And it's interesting." I opened it.

Dear Hank,

Mrs. Mary Ellen Dickinson presented in the ophthamology clinic on 10/13/56. You, of course, are acquainted with her history. Her chief complaint was "My eye falls out of my head." This complaint was unique, to say the least, but she was able to verify her statement.

(I should state here that I called in all of the ophthamology residents for the uniqueness of her performance.)

Work-up consisted of the usual visual and ophthamological examinations. Positive findings were a decrease in visual acuity on the right with some muscle weakness and eye deviation. (Reports enclosed.)

X-rays revealed the cause of her difficulty to be a shallow eye bone socket that did not allow the globe to "seat'" sufficiently.

Treatment consisted of sewing together the lateral aspect of her eyelids (0.5 cms). I hope this solves her problem.

I thank you for allowing me to participate in the care of this pleasant woman with a most unusual condition.

Sincerely,

Dr. Wayne Podderno

EPILOGUE

The doctors at the University of Chicago had succeeded in putting an end to Mary Ellen's eye making exits from her head. I saw her in the office about six months after her lid surgery. She brought her husband in who had flu symptoms. And although the lids of her right eye were sewn partly shut, her vision seemed to be just fine.

She told me that she was happy that her falling eye problem had been corrected.

But I think she was even happier that her bridge club had resumed its meetings.

Dad on an outing with the kids. (L-R): Joyce, Suzy, David & Daniel. (Mom was the photographer.)

MISS HALLEY- PART ONE

Ruth Ann Halley R.N. was forty-eight years old when the Coronary Care Unit was organized at Gary's St. Mary Mercy Medical Center. One had to be sure to refer to her as Miss Halley. Not Ruth Ann. And definitely not Mrs. Halley. She insisted on being addressed only as "Miss Halley"...always. "I've never been a Missus and I never intend to be." That was Miss Halley's rejoinder to anyone who ever referred to her as a married woman.

No, there was no mistake about it. She was nobody's Missus. She was Miss Ruth Ann Halley, R.N...a graduate of an old line Catholic School of Nursing that was run with a good deal of strict military style discipline. The approach to nursing education experienced by Miss Halley and her classmates there was strictly "by-the-book." It worked something like this: First, the Doctor was the indisputable top dog; as infallible in his profession as the Pope was in his. Secondly, perpetual virginity was much esteemed and lauded — to be guarded, protected, and defended. (And Miss Halley was obedient.) And finally, patients—all patients—were to be treated with kindness, but firmness; for the reason that patients really had no idea whatsoever what was best for them.

Miss Halley had worked competently through the several years as a general floor nurse. But when she heard that the hospital was organizing a Coronary Care Unit, she volunteered to become a member of the initial cadre of Intensive Care Nursing Specialists. I was in charge of organizing the new unit, which was initially conceived to care for cardiac as well as other acutely ill patients. Therefore, I was given the prerogative of interviewing the nursing candidates.

I didn't want Miss Halley.

Like I said, she was a fairly competent floor nurse. But I outlined my reasons for rejecting her in a letter to the Director of Nursing who was a gentle and kind nun—Sister Margaret—who ran her department with more heart than logic. In the letter, I cited Miss Halley's distaste for "the electrical junk" (EKG monitors, IV pumps, etc.), her inability to respond adequately in emergencies, and her obsession in doing things exactly by the book. She had no understanding of the need to occasionally be flexible in differing situations. The letter was a well-organized, three page submission of why Miss Halley would be a most unsuitable candidate to become a Nursing Specialist in the new unit.

I never considered the possibility that I would be overruled. But Sister Margaret had veto power over my recommendations. (Could it have had anything to do with the fact that Sister Margaret and Miss Halley were in the same nursing class?)

"Dr. Kamen," Sister Margaret began. "Miss Halley was a top student in Nursing School. All A's. Always! And she never went out with boys. Never!" (I didn't find that difficult to believe.) Obviously, in Sister Margaret's mind, the latter qualified Miss Halley for sainthood, and my plea to omit Miss Halley from the new class was unsuccessful. OK Miss Halley, you're in, and I'll just make the best of it.

From the start, Miss Halley was a poor student when it came to learning how to run the electrocardiograph. I assigned special tutors to help her recognize abnormal cardiac rhythms and evidence of heart damage. The tutors were mostly patient with her, but the process was painful, and still she showed few signs of measurable progress. When she was taught how to monitor and respond to rapid changes in vital signs, the tutors would inevitably hear; "This isn't the way I was taught in Nursing School."

Both the tutors and I counseled her repeatedly to withdraw from the program, but her response was to repeatedly run to Sister Margaret for defense and consolation. Sister Margaret still had veto power and used it. Miss Halley was going to be a part of the new unit despite my strong objections.

The first time the unit opened was a Monday morning. In a brief ceremony, the unit was blessed by the hospital Chaplain as community leaders and hospital VIP's looked on. Miss Halley was there too. She was working the first shift of the first day. I wasn't at all surprised when catastrophe struck just six hours later.

The first patient admitted to the new unit was Mr. James Farrell. James was the head of the local beer and liquor distributing company. His trucks bearing the name "Farrell & Sons--Miller High Life Distributors" were seen throughout Northwest Indiana. He was a rich and powerful figure in the community. He was also a member of the Board of Trustees of St. Mary Medical Center. So we were, or course, eager to impress. But there really wasn't anything to worry about. Everything was in place. Looking around the room, the sparkling clean unit hummed with high-tech efficiency and state of the art electronic equipment. I was there, along with the hospital administrator to greet him as he came through the door. Miss Halley was there too. Was there really anything to worry about?

James Farrell came to the unit after having experienced severe chest pain early that morning. The pain was strong enough that it woke him. He was examined at his home by his neighbor, an internist who admitted James to our just-opened unit.

Miss Halley put the patient into bed and made sure that he was comfortable. I watched as she applied the electrocardiograph leads from the heart monitor to his chest. She gave him his dose of morphine for the pain, then she turned her attention to the TV like screen monitor and kept her eyes riveted there, watching each electrical heart impulse as it appeared on the screen. She literally didn't miss a beat.

Perhaps I had misjudged her. Everything she had done thus far was correct and efficient. No need to worry. With Farrell tucked safely into bed, I left the unit and visited my hospitalized patients. No need to worry. (If I said it enough times, perhaps I'd start to really believe it.) She'll do just fine. I'd have to write an apology to Sister Margaret.

Then suddenly in mid-afternoon, the STAT page and alarm sounded.

"Dr. Kamen to ICU STAT! Dr. Kamen to ICU STAT!"

I was on the fifth floor. The Coronary Care Unit was on the first. I ran down the stairs, through the hall and into the unit through the double doors. The scene inside was near bedlam.

Mr. Farrell was out of his bed. He was screaming, swearing, and then screaming again. Wire leads to the EKG monitor were still attached to his chest. Profanities poured from his mouth endlessly, and he was wildly waving his arms. He had his sights set on the double doors, and he was trying to flee the unit, but was restrained by two orderlies and a nurse.

Miss Halley was standing in the middle of the room saying repeatedly: "I did what was right! I saved him! I did what was right!"

All was seemingly coming apart.

It was only after much coaxing and persuasion that the staff was able to get Mr. Farrell back into his bed.

"I'm going home! I'm getting out of this asylum! Give me my pants! Somebody get me my pants! I'm going home! I don't care if I die, I'd rather go home than be killed in here! I'm getting out of here NOW!"

"Mr. Farrell," I said. "Let me find out what happened first. I can see that you're quite upset. Just let me see what happened. Give me five minutes. That's all, Mr. Farrell. Just five minutes!"

"Look, doctor, I don't give a shit what you find out. That BITCH (pointing to Miss Halley) tried to kill me and I'm getting OUT OF HERE!"

"Please, Mr. Farrell. Just give me five minutes. Please."

He didn't answer me. I assumed that meant I had bought myself the five minutes. I motioned to Miss Halley, who was now seated at the chart desk, to follow me into the Family Consultation Room. I closed the door.

"Please, Miss Halley. Tell me what happened. I want to know everything."

"Well, Dr. Kamen, I did everything that I was taught to do. I did everything right and I saved him, so I don't see all the fuss."

"Tell me everything, Miss Halley."

"Well, you know how you trained us to spot abnormal rhythms?"

"Yes."

"Well, he's got an abnormal rhythm. See, I even made a printout. Look at the strip."

I looked at the electrocardiogram. I looked at the paper again, and then back at Miss Halley.

"Uh, Miss Halley, this is not an abnormal rhythm. It's an artifact. Do you remember those? Remember how we taught you that this is what happens when one of the electrodes on the patient's chest comes off? It's just an artifact, Miss Halley."

"Oh. Uh...are you sure?"

"Yes."

"Oh."

"Well, what happened then, after you saw the strip, Miss Halley?" I really didn't want to hear her answer, because I knew what happened.

"Well, Dr. Kamen, I thought he had ventricular fibrillation...you know...the rhythm that you taught us that kills the patient immediately?"

"Yes." I was now certain that I didn't want to hear anymore.

"Yes, well, you know what the treatment for that is."

Uh-oh. It was coming.

Miss Halley continued. "You shock the patient and I did. I gave him the full 400 volts across his chest. " A long pause. "I did it twice."

The nightmare was real. I sat there in stunned silence while I thought of what to do next.

"Miss Halley, how did Mr. Farrell look before you shocked him? What was he doing?"

"Well, Dr. Kamen, Mr. Farrell was reading the newspaper when it happened."

Suddenly, my voice became involuntarily shrill. "Miss Halley, how in heaven's name could he have ventricular fibrillation with no output from his heart if he's reading a newspaper? If you have ventricular fibrillation, you're out! You're unconscious! You're about dead! There's no pulse! There's not anything! Nothing! You are not reading a newspaper!"

"Yes, I remember that now."

"Well?"

"Well what, Dr. Kamen?"

"Well what happened after that?"

"Well, it's like I told you. I saw the rhythm and then went to the bedside and hooked up the defibrillator and applied the conductive gel to his chest and..."

"Wait, what was Mr. Farrell doing by this time?"

"Well, he put down his newspaper and asked me what I was doing."

"Didn't the fact that he was coherent give you a hint that he was OK?"

"Well, Dr. Kamen, I told him that everything was going to be alright and that I was going to take good care of him."

"Then?"

"Well, then I thought I'd put the paddles on his chest and assured him that everything was going to be alright. He was looking at everything I was doing, you know."

"I'll bet. And then?"

"And then I zapped him. I gave him all it had."

Stunned.

"And then?"

"Well, his eyes got real wide...you know...like bug-eyed. He was of course jerking all over the bed and stuff. It was real violent there for awhile. And then he just kept jerking for awhile longer...his hair was getting all mussed and everything. Then he started mumbling..and then he started screaming real loud."

"And then?"

"Well then I looked at the EKG to see if my defibrillation was successful—you know, just like you taught us—but the monitor looked the same as it did before." She paused. A long pause. Finally: "Then I zapped him again."

She zapped him a second time. Don't do anything rash, I told myself. Just remain calm and think about this for a minute. She zapped him a second time...no, there could be no mistake about it...this was real...it had happened...to a hospital board member in the first hours after the birth of the unit...and by a woman who had confessed months ago that she didn't like "the electrical junk" and that was to be an integral part of the job for which she had volunteered. She zapped him a second time.

"Dr. Kamen?"

"Yes, Miss Halley?"

"I think you should know that when finally he stopped jerking after the second volt, he became rather incoherent because then he jumped out of bed and started screaming...you know obscenities and everything...and, uh, I think that's just about the time that you came down."

After a few minutes, I got up, poured some coffee, asked Miss Halley if she wanted any and she said no...that she only drank coffee on her official coffee break or lunch hour. Then I turned, and left Miss Halley in the consultation room and went back to Mr. Farrell in the unit.

Mr. Farrell appeared to be somewhat calmer He had received some more morphine and a barbiturate while I was in the consultation room. But he was still mumbling.

"Well, Mr. Farrell," I began in a positive tone of voice. "I think I understand what happened, and believe me, it won't be repeated."

108

"You're goddam right it won't be repeated, because I'm getting the hell out of here." Mr. Farrell's words erupted in torrents. "I'm laying here, reading my paper peacefully, not bothering nobody when this so-called nurse...this...this...witch, starts smearing me with gel and the next thing I know, I'm seeing ten thousand bolts of lightning in my head and I'm convulsing all over the bed here...and shittin' Doc...I'm shittin' right here in the bed and Holy God my chest is on fire...and my pecker is tingling and vibrating. So I holler 'HELP!' and what does she do? She does the same goddam thing all over again! I couldn't believe it! The bitch didn't kill me the first time, so she's gonna try again. Is that how it goes around here Doc?"

"Of course not Mr. Farrell, but I certainly understand how you feel."

"Aw just screw her and screw you too. Screw the hospital while you're at it...I want out of here and I want out NOW!"

Mr. Farrell dressed and left the hospital against medical advice.

EPILOGUE

Mr. Farrell recovered uneventfully at home, and his doctor refused to admit any more of his patients to the unit for several months.

Sister Margaret, informed by me in detail of the events that took place that first day in the unit, refused to transfer Miss Halley out of the unit. She explained that I had "demonstrated to Miss Halley what she did wrong, and I doubt the episode will ever be repeated. It was a marvelous learning experience not only for Miss Halley but for everyone on the unit."

Overruled yet again. But it was only a temporary setback. Miss Halley was to remain on the ICU unit for only two months more, then she was forced out by even more bizarre behavior. Miss Halley definitely had a "screw" loose. Turn the page and keep reading.

THE RETURN OF MISS HALLEY

Miss Ruth Ann Halley, R.N. was introduced in the previous chapter. In summary, she was weird. But there were signs of psychiatric disturbances even before the "Mr. Farrell Gets Fried" incident. Let me give you just a brief personality profile based on the observances of those who worked with her.

Miss Halley was definitely a loner. She kept to herself, speaking to others only when spoken to first, and then only if the conversation pertained to her professional duties. She never became too close to any of her patients, always preferring to remain emotionally detached. As the years progressed, she became increasingly obsessive in her work habits. For example, she would repeatedly check, recheck, and then check again procedures which she performed routinely— including blood pressure, pulse and temperature measurements. She measured urine output to the one-fiftieth of an ounce and then poured it into another beaker to measure again. When she was criticized, regardless of its nature, she bristled with anger and indignation. When she was praised for a job particularly well done, she ignored the compliment.

Just two or three weeks before she joined the Intensive Care cadre of nurses, it was widely rumored, (then later confirmed), that she was gay, and living with a much younger recent nursing school graduate. The younger nurse never made a secret of her sexual preference, and was open and honest about her relationship with Miss Halley.

But just after the "Zapping" episode, Miss Halley's mental condition seemed to rapidly deteriorate. Physicians complained to me, as Unit Director, about her ceaseless and mostly unnecessary phone calls at all hours. As an example, she called one doctor close to 1:00am to inform him that, "your patient has just had a beautiful bowel movement," even though the singular event, as "spectacular" as it was, was unrelated to the patient's ailment.

Frequently, Miss Halley would remain at the hospital for one or two hours after her shift ended to go over her charting word for word. During shift change reports, she would ramble on and on to the incoming shift about each patient's condition—even reporting such minutiae as "he left a tiny portion of scrambled eggs on his plate...I think it must have been burned a little or maybe it had too much salt on it, or maybe he just didn't want anymore...I'm really not sure...what do you think?"

But when it came to the technical essentials of a patient's events, she would often gloss over them or even ignore them. She would hesitate to discuss a patient's EKG rhythm changes or patterns, the state of hydration, electrolyte balance or other "new-fangled electro-technical" patient conditions. The other nurses incessantly complained to me about her idiosyncrasies. Finally, in frustration and desperation, I met with Sister Margaret yet again, and BEGGED her to transfer Miss Halley out of the unit. But Sister Margaret was ready with her answer.

"Look, Dr. Kamen, I'm running nursing. You're running the ICU. I don't interfere with YOU!"

"But Sister!" I pleaded. "I can't RUN the ICU without top nurses! Let's face it! Miss Halley just doesn't have what it takes to be a part of the ICU nursing team! She's tearing it apart! She just can't handle it!"

Sister Margaret projected a cold and penetrating stare.

"I am running the nursing service for this hospital Dr. Kamen. That's all. Good day!"

And so it went. I continued , however to document Miss Halley's bizarre behavior on the unit. Sister Margaret continued to ignore it. But on Christmas Eve of that year, she could ignore the obvious no longer. Miss Halley would finally implode.

I was just about finished with my rounds and was busy doing some paper work in my office when suddenly the pager sounded: "Dr. Kamen...Dr.Kamen...Please come to ICU at your convenience." The voice belonged to Eleanor Savitch, an astute charge nurse on the unit. I called her to find out what was going on.

"Oh, no real problem, Doctor," she said. "The patient in bed one just expired and I thought you'd like to pronounce him before you went home."

The death of the elderly gentleman in bed one had been expected. He had been admitted to the ICU after being operated on for a ruptured thoracic aortic aneurysm. The effort was heroic, but the surgery could not be satisfactorily completed. Almost the entire aorta had split.

I dropped by the unit about a half hour later and performed the routine final examination. The were no respirations, no pulse, and the EKG was flat. (No cardiac activity). His skin was cool and clammy and the pupils were fixed and dilated. I took the patient's chart and made the following notation: "Patient expired. Pronounced dead at 2:42 p.m. 12/24. (Signed) Jack M. Kamen, M.D."

As I was writing, I heard someone enter the desk area. It was Miss Halley. She had come in for duty on the three to eleven shift. She greeted me in her typically cold and perfunctory manner. It was no wonder. After all, the fact that I didn't want her on the unit was no secret. I considered the unit "mine" and she was definitely an unwanted, incompetent intruder. I acknowledged her greeting and went home early.

I was looking forward to going home. It was a rare evening for me to be home with my family with no interruptions. We had planned an early dinner together...an infrequent occurrence throughout most of the year. But everything seemed quiet in the ICU. There were no patient calls and only essential personnel were on duty. It was Christmas Eve. I locked up and went home.

Dinner was relaxed and delicious. At about 8 o'clock I got into bed, propped up with three or four pillows, and for the first time in weeks, pulled a non-medical book off the bookshelf and prepared to enjoy the murder mystery I bought months before, but hadn't had a chance to read. I opened the book to the Preface. Ah-h-h-h. This was heavenly. Then...

The phone rang.

One—two—three rings. I knew I had to answer it, but I delayed doing so as long as possible. Whatever or whoever it was, I had a gut feeling that it meant an abrupt end to my relaxation. Experience is the best teacher. I picked it up.

"Yes?" The more traditional "hello" would have been too accommodating to whoever was responsible for stealing my moment of bliss.

"This is Miss Halley." (Was this a curse?)

"Yes?"

"Dr. Kamen, you know the patient in bed one? The one you wrote in the chart had expired?"

"Yes, of course."

"Well, Dr. Kamen, I just called to tell you he isn't dead."

An immediate response was impossible. I became totally confused and couldn't immediately process what I'd heard.

"Dr. Kamen, are you still there?" Miss Halley inquired.

I could not answer.

"Dr. Kamen?" she began to speak more loudly. Finally—

114

"Yes, I'm here."

"Well, Dr. Kamen, Mr. Powolski is not dead." Her tone was triumphant.

I thought an explanation on her part was appropriate at this point.

"What do you mean, Miss Halley? Exactly what do you mean 'he's not dead'?"

" I mean exactly what I said, Dr. Kamen. HE'S NOT DEAD!"

"Did you feel a pulse? Did you hear a heartbeat Miss Halley?"

"No."

"Did you reapply his EKG?"

"Yes."

"Does he have an EKG complex?"

"I don't think so, but I can't be really sure because of what happened with Mr. Farrell. Do you remember?"

"Yes, I remember, Miss Halley. Now tell me, why do you think he's not dead?"

"Because..." There was a long, protracted intentional hesitation here. "Because he sat up in bed. Bolted upright."

I was dumbfounded.

"He did WHAT?"

"I believe you heard me Dr. Kamen."

"Yes, I did, but I want to hear it again."

"I said he bolted upright in his bed. Just sat right up."

"OK. Then what did he do?"

"Well, then he looked around and then he laid back down again."

"That's all?"

"Well, isn't that enough, Dr. Kamen?"

"Did he speak to you?"

"No."

"Alright Miss Halley. When did this happen?"

"A few minutes before I called you."

"Miss Halley, let me speak to any of the other nurses on the unit with you."

Her response was one of indignation.

"Dr. Kamen! Mr. Powolski is MY patient. Mine and mine alone! No one else's! Mine!!!"

That she became indignant alarmed me. Miss Halley was many things, but she was not one to ignore or deny a doctor's request. I realized then that her mind had decompensated.

"Alright, thank you Miss Halley. I'll get back to you."

"But Dr. Kamen, I think you should come down and reevaluate Mr. Powolski and start new treatment. Or I'll call Dr. Thompson, his attending doctor. He'll know what to do for sure."

Damn. First, that episode with Mr. Farrell almost being electrocuted to death, and now this! I had called Thompson earlier in the day to tell him that his patient had died. He thanked me for saving him the trip. I told the family. They cried, but were accepting of his passing, as it had been imminent for some time. I was sure they were home by now. For all I knew, the funeral director could have been on his way. And why not? It had been two hours since I pronounced him dead.

"Uh, Miss Halley...has the funeral home contacted you?"

"Oh no. Don't worry, Dr. Kamen. They called immediately before I called you. I just told them not to come because he was still alive."

Oh my God!

"Miss Halley, do you remember who the Funeral Director is?"

"Sure. It is Murray and Olsen."

"OK, I'll get back to you."

I grabbed the telephone book. Let's see..Funeral Directors...no. Funeral Homes...no. Ah yes, Funeral services. Here we are. Barker...Carruthers...Falmouth & Jones... here it is...Murray and Olsen. Got it.

I dialed the number of Murray and Olsen. A voice that sounded like it belonged to someone who had been fast asleep answered.

"Uh...yeah...uh...hello?"

"Hello? Is this Murray and Olsen?"

"Uh, yes. Murray and Olsen. We meet your needs in your hours of need. Ted Murray speaking. How can I help you?"

Oh good. It was Ted. I knew him.

"Ted, this is Dr. Kamen. Jack Kamen. I don't have a lot of time to explain, but I believe you got a call about a patient of mine in the ICU over at Gary Mercy...a Powolski...and..."

"Oh yeah! Hey Doc, this is gonna sound crazy, but a nurse just called and said he's not..."

"Wait Ted. Let me finish. There's been this small misunderstanding."

"You call this 'small' Doc? First a guy is dead and then..."

"No Ted, wait. He's dead, but..." I didn't know how to proceed from here. On the one hand, I could tell him that this wacky nurse in our ICU unit had been imagining things. No. Think again, Jack. How would that look to admit to having a deranged, incompetent nurse on duty in a place where all the patients are in critical condition? Then the answer suddenly came to me.

"He's dead, Ted. But it's just that the paperwork isn't complete yet."

"You mean he's not pronounced?"

"Uh, Ted, I'll tell you what. We'll get back to you. You, uh, haven't told the family about the nurse's call, have you?"

"No, not yet. But I was going to call a little later."

"Please Ted, don't call anyone until I get back to you. OK?"

"Sure Doc. OK."

I was relieved. I hung up, then dialed the hospital switchboard and asked to speak to the nursing supervisor, Sister Margaret. They had her paged. She knew why I was calling when she answered the phone.

"Hello, Dr. Kamen. Now before you say anything, I am going to have Miss Halley transferred out of the unit, but in the meantime, you'll have to come down here to re-pronounce Mr. Powolski."

"Wait a minute Sister," I said. "Why do I have to come down to pronounce him again? He's dead, Sister. D-E-A-D. Dead! There! I pronounced him!" I was angry now. Angry and frustrated to think that I had to be a party to this lunacy. "He's not going to be any more dead if I come down there than if I'm telling you over the phone. He's just plain Dead!!! Stone cold dead!!!

"Dr. Kamen, look. I understand that he's dead too, but since Miss Halley wrote on the patient's chart that he bolted upright in his bed, we cannot release the body. What would happen if someone looked over the chart, saw the notation that he sat up after being pronounced dead, and he wasn't re-examined? We'd get fried!"

"OK. OK, I'll be there to chart it first thing in the morning."

"Dr. Kamen, I'm really very sorry about this, but we just can't release the body until..."

"Yeah, yeah. Isn't there anyone else in the house?"

"Are you kidding? It's Christmas Eve."

"I know, Sister. I know. OK."

Outside, a steady snow was falling, turning the world white. Through the flurries, Christmas lights twinkled and shone on the houses I passed as I made my way back to the hospital. There was only a rare car on the road as I made the twenty minute drive. Things were quiet and peaceful.

When I arrived at the unit, I found that Miss Halley had already been assigned to non-patient nursing duties on a regular medical floor. Another nurse was standing at Mr. Powolski's bedside.

"Gee, Dr., I'm really sorry you had to come all the way back here tonight. He's dead you know."

"Yeah. I know."

EPILOGUE

Now it's quite possible that you were thinking while you were reading this story that I, in fact, had pronounced Mr. Powolski dead in error. While I do acknowledge that this happens, (very rarely), Mr. Powolski was indeed as dead the first time he was pronounced as he was the second time around.

Miss Halley would never again return to work at the hospital. She was determined by the nursing service to be emotionally unstable and incapable of discharging her nursing duties. She obtained a job a couple of weeks later as an industrial nurse at a local garment manufacturing plant. I never saw her again...except when she still pops up now and then in my nightmares.

HELDA

1948.

The sparse remnants of European Jewry continued to trickle into post-World War II America, Canada, or the newly formed State of Israel...to any sanctuary where they could find peace and escape from the horrific nightmare that was Hitler's panacea for redeeming Germany: Nazism and the eradication of the entire Jewish race. In America, they were "displaced persons" (DP's)....an apt appellation—for where indeed did they—where could they— belong?

They were displaced world wanderers, uprooted and betrayed by their native homeland by a demon so vicious it would much sooner deliver rights to rodents than to Jews...men, women and children. Those who came to America found, however, that they did indeed have rights here, and that began with the recognition of their humanity. They were someone. Here, they could begin to rebuild what was left of their lives. Here, they could light the Sabbath candles in peace and worship in the synagogue. But could they ever learn to trust again?

They came to America homeless, penniless, with not much more than the clothes they were wearing, and perhaps, the memory of a life that had virtually ceased to exist.

Where to begin? Most soon learned that their greatest opportunities could be found in America's large, industrialized cities where jobs and housing were plentiful. The sights were amazing. America's big cities looked and felt nothing like the little "shtetls" (small isolated Jewish communities) they had left, but least in the shtetl, life was predictable. Everyone knew each other and there were few surprises. Their world stopped and started within the shtetl's borders. This...this America...was overwhelming.

The new immigrants soon realized that the task of becoming a self-sufficient American included learning how to fit in—how to become "Americanized"—how to look and act like real "Yankees." With most of their families exterminated during the war, the only familial customs they had to rely on were religious, learned long ago in the shtetl. How could these refugees fit among the skyscrapers, the glitzy stores, the vast homes, and huge factories? A new life in America. Now it was to be home.

"Hey, Yankel!" Our clinical instructor at the Mount Sinai Hospital latched on to my Yiddish name on my first day in my third year in the out-patient clinic. My friend Lester insisted on calling me "Yankel." Good ol' Lester. His goal was to be a psychiatrist. Because he was a student of the old, ultraconservative Freudian school of psychiatry, where the psychoanalyst only listened. He had diagnosed a patient with urinary retention related to prostate enlargement as being unable to urinate because he was "stingy." This was so, he told the patient, because his mother used to reward him for producing a bowel movement when he was five years old.

"Yankel!" the supervisor, who was also Jewish, called. "I've got a patient for you and only for you. You're the only one here who knows Bubbe Lushen. (Meaning "grandmother's Language" or Yiddish.) We've got a Jewish DP who needs glasses. Give her the routine and then we'll send her to Frankel." (An ophthalmologist.)

The "routine." You need to understand what that meant. Simply stated, if you were unfortunate enough to have to come into a medical school's teaching clinic, then you would have to undergo the "routine," regardless of the nature of your complaint. In 1948, that involved a comprehensive physical — including a urinalysis and blood tests. It also meant that every orifice of your body would be invaded. The "routine" physical was important because it gave students such as myself hands-on experience. So it was that I entered the examining cubicle, met Helda Weiner, and prepared to give her the "routine", though she had come in only to get a prescription for eyeglasses.

Helda's face had a fearful, yet quizzical look. Her head tilted slightly as she looked at me. But she perked up noticeably when she heard my first words in Yiddish to her. At last! At last! Someone who could understand her! Someone who would set everything straight.

Helda appeared to be in her late thirties but her chart indicated that she was twenty-nine. She sat on the examination table already gowned in a too-short open backed robe that forced her to salvage a degree of dignity by sitting with her legs tightly crossed so that she could at least half-cover her buttocks.

"I don't think they understand." she began, at first in a broken staccato Yiddish. It was difficult to follow what she was saying.

"In fact, they don't understand at all," she continued in Yiddish. "I came for my eyes. My eyes! MY EYES!" She pointed forcefully at her eyes as she spoke. "I can't read any documents. Everything is blurry unless I hold the paper real close. I need glasses. That is all. Do you understand? The Jewish Agency sent me here for glasses. That is all I need."

She had a look on her face that said, "This is nothing like the shtetl." Back in the shtetl, if you had trouble with your vision, you would go to the store there and try on spectacles until things looked clearer. You were rarely (if ever) sent for an examination. But here in America, a big city America, for all your medical care—including spectacles—you had to drag yourself to Mount Sinai Hospital, on the west side, in the heart of the largest concentration of Jews in the city.

She came for a pair of glasses. I knew that. But I also knew that I had to give her the "routine." It was required. Now, how could I explain this to Helda? Start with the basics.

"Now Helda," I began hesitatingly in Yiddish. "The nurses DO understand, and they did the right thing by having you undress to get ready."

"Ready? Ready for what?"

I could have used another course in medical school here. Why didn't they teach a class in "doctor-patient talk"?

"Well, Miss Weiner,"

"It's MRS. Weiner." she corrected. "My husband Shmuel, may he rest in peace..." She didn't finish.

"Alright Mrs. Weiner. Let me explain. I know you are having trouble with your eyes, but did you know that there are many things that can make the eyes bad?"

"They were bad in Europe and I had glasses there and they were alright for me. But I lost them, so now..."

"Yes, but still there are many things that can make the eyes bad." She was much more attentive now. I felt buoyed. "Like diabetes or high blood pressure and...and..." Damn. I couldn't think of any more. Luckily I didn't have to because she interrupted.

"Yes, I see."

"Yes, so we have to do a complete examination to see if anything else is wrong and then you not only get your glasses, but then you know you're healthy!"

Now she was beaming.

"Yes, yes, I see. Alright. Examine my heart and for my blood pressure."

Uh-oh.

"Well, that's fine Mrs. Weiner, but we have to examine everything."

Her brow furrowed and her head tilted. The quizzical look on her face returned.

"Everything?"

"Well yes, Mrs. Weiner. We want to make absolutely sure you're healthy."

Warily, she allowed me to begin, but she watched me intently. It was clear that she didn't completely trust me. Never mind that I spoke Yiddish and was able to communicate easily with her. She just didn't have full trust.

After each system was examined, she echoed again and again the nature of her visit: "I came here because of my eyes. My eyes! It's my eyes! When are you going to look at my eyes?"

I explained that the routine was to examine the part that the patient complained of last. That's a safeguard so we don't miss anything along the way.

She didn't like the word "routine." She had an expression of disgust every time the word came up in our conversation. I guessed it was because the word "routine" reminded her of how good the Germans were at their "routines."

The nurse, named Golda, who was assisting me in the cubicle as I examined Mrs. Weiner, could understand nothing of what was being said. Though she was also Jewish, she was a third generation Jew, and so no Yiddish was spoken in her home. My parents had come from Poland to America, so they spoke Yiddish almost exclusively in our home.

As I proceeded with the examination, Golda jotted down my findings on Helda's chart as we progressed. The examination of the ears, nose, and throat was rapid except for the palpation of the

125

tongue (for lumps) which she had never before heard of. "Du bist mishugeh!" (You're crazy!) was all she could say when that particular procedure was completed.

Listening to Helda's breath sounds was uneventful—unlike the breast examination. She insisted that every part of her body be covered with a sheet except for the two square inches I was palpating. But she resolutely would not allow her nipples to be exposed, even though I needed to check for dimpling.

Then a look at Helda's left arm stunned. I had never seen a concentration camp tattoo. There it was, everything—the long train rides in fetid cattle cars —the gas chambers—the crematoriums—the lampshades of human skin and other horrors and atrocities— all came rushing into my mind at the sight of the bluish-purple number on Helda's arm. They were no longer the accounts and exposes that appeared in the newspapers, magazines, or the newsreels in the local theaters, or on the radio. They were real. Helda's arm bore testimony to the suffering, the torture and the death of millions.

It was several seconds later before I could come back to the reality of the examination cubicle. Ironically, Helda was more cheerful and talkative than she had been. She chatted with giggles and staccato laughter of what she was planning to do...her new job...her new home.

Suddenly, Helda sat vertically up on the table. "Can I get my glasses now?"

How was I to explain what was next? To aggravate matters even more, I didn't know the Yiddish words for "pelvic examination." My folks, after all, never had the occasion to discuss this. (Or if they did, they never did so in front of the "kids.") The best I could do was to explain that with Golda's help, I had to examine her nether-regions.

"My what?" came her swift reply.

"Well, you know Mrs. Weiner, your bottom part."

"You want to see my taches (e.g. ass)?"

All rapidly deteriorated. Horrible. Golda gently asked me what was going on when she saw the horror on Helda's face. I explained the situation. Golda had years of experience in the outpatient clinic and had developed a phrase that appeared to be soothing to the patients:

"It's nothing! Absolutely nothing!"

But with Helda? Slowly and gently...very gently...Golda pushed Helda's body back until she lay flat on the table.

"Please, go out for two minutes, Doctor," said Golda.

I was glad for the temporary respite. As I stood outside the cubicle, I noticed that my hands were sweating. I involuntarily sighed. But too soon, the door opened.

"OK," said Golda. "You can come in now."

I walked in and saw that Helda was positioned for the pelvic examination. Her buttocks were poised at the edge of the table and her legs were in the stirrups.

"Just tell me what you are going to do," she said nervously.

"Uh...I'm just going to examine you."

"Is this how I get my glasses?"

"Uh...well...I'm just going to examine you." (How could this get any worse?)

Helda had her knees tightly clamped together. I repeated Golda's words to Helda:

"It's nothing. Absolutely nothing."

As I spoke, the nurse began to pry her knees apart. She wouldn't spread them as far as was really necessary, but it was enough so that I could at least begin. I could have begun, except that I was immobile by then. Immobile. It took Golda to bring me back.

"Dr. Kamen, put on your gloves! Doctor, get it over with!"

She knew exactly what I was thinking.

"Just tell me what you are going to do!" Helda was angry.

"I'm just going to examine you." I repeated. "It's nothing. Absolutely nothing." Regardless, Helda appeared to calm down. I was gloved and ready to proceed.

Golda stood at the end of the table with her right shoulder against one of Helda's knees and her left hand pushing against the other knee. By this maneuver, she was able to maintain an opening. With her right hand, she squirted some lubricant on my index finger. Ready.

What happened next is something of a blur.

I began to insert my finger into her rectum. She immediately screamed. No need to interpret here. The entire personnel of the outpatient department came running into the cubicle. Helda began shrieking and alternately screaming in Yiddish:

"What kind of country is this America? Aa-a-a-gh! What kind? Tell me what kind?!!! Aa-a-a-gh!!! What has my ass got to do with my eyes? I see with my eyes! Not with my ass! Do people in America see through their asses? My "dreck" (feces) is fine! My eyes aren't! It's my eyes! My eyes!!!!!!!!"

With that, and with astonishing speed, Helda jerked her heels out of the stirrups and got off the table, swooped up her clothes and ran out of the clinic. Barefooted, bare-bottomed, she ran out screaming the same words over and over:

"It's my eyes! MY EYES! What? What? What has my ass got to do with my eyes? America! Feh! They're all Meshugeh (crazy)!"

EPILOGUE

This whole episode was gut-wrenching. Our clinical instructor left the area as soon as all the students had begun their assignments. He would not return to discuss each case until near the period's end. As a third-year medical extern, I was not allowed to change any examination protocol without his specific permission. I certainly would have...if I could have.

I assume Helda finally got her glasses, though I don't know that with certainty. She never returned to the clinic. Though I've been in practice now for decades, I'm still at a loss of how I could have answered her questions: "Do people in America see through their asses?" Well, at times, perhaps...especially when it comes to politics. And "What has my ass got to do with my eyes?" Now that I think about it, there is an answer. You see, your ass and your eyes, Helda, are both a part of the "routine." But it's nothing. Absolutely nothing.

MICHAEL

After med school, I interned at Chicago's Cook County Hospital. The institution was a behemoth structure located on the city's west side. It was, to many, the sole method of receiving any medical care.

The internship was strongly sought. One had to compete for a spot through a series of written and oral exams. What made an internship at Cook County so desirable? Because while there, one was certain to see most everything and do most everything there was to see and do in world of medicine as it existed in 1952. The gamut of human illnesses passed unceasingly through the hospital doors. During any i4-hour shift in the ER, an average of 300 patients were seen by each intern. There were two interns always on duty. One case seemed to flow into the next with names, faces, and complaints becoming a blur by day's end.

But my work and experiences at Cook County Hospital were of immeasurable help in my practice at the Indiana Harbor Clinic. As in any of life's experiences however, there always seems to be something that happens that leaves one stunned and at a complete loss to react logically. Such experiences are not easily forgotten. And so it was with Michael.

I was at the clinic when I received a call from the East Chicago Hospital ER nurse. It was a typical grimy, sooty, sweaty, dirty day. I picked up the phone.

"Dr. Kamen?"

"Yes?"

"Uh...you're on the staff now?"

"Yes." I had been accepted as a staff member the previous day.

"Well, you're on call. Well actually you're not, but we can't find anyone else."

I was to l quickly learn that it was common practice at Indiana Harbor to pass off the most undesirable (non-paying) patients to the newest doctor on the staff.

"Nobody wants him, Dr. Kamen."

"Well, OK. What have you got?"

"You've got to come over Dr. Kamen. And take a look at the x-ray."

"I'm on my way."

My office at Indiana Harbor was empty and I was eagerly seeking patients to start. I left the office and ten minutes later I entered the hospital ER. I found the nurses huddled in a corner with an x-ray on the lighted view box. As I got closer, it wasn't hard to see what was going on. It took a while, however, for me to fully comprehend what I was seeing. But there it was...plainly and unmistakably on the x-ray.

There was a fishhook in the patient's urinary bladder.

I stared at the film. One of the nurses came and stood next to me.

"Well," I said. "It's a fish hook."

"Very good, Dr. Kamen."

"It looks to be about 3/4 of an inch long."

"You must have graduated at the top of your class." (Later on I learned to like her.)

"How do you think it got..." I didn't get to finish my question.

"Why don't you ask him? He's in five. Name's Michael Hanks."

I walked over to cubicle five and pulled the curtain aside. The man on the examination table was obviously in severe pain. There was no doubt about that. His face was pale and ghost-like. He was sweating as he leaned back on the table on his elbows, his face contorted by pain.

"Hello. I'm Dr. Kamen. How did the..."

"Please Doc. Don't ask me that. Just get it out!"

It was apparent that further questioning of how a fish hook ended up in his bladder would be futile. I pulled up the sheet. Protruding from Michael's penis was three inches of single strand nylon fishline. (The fishline itself, not radiopaque, could not be seen on the x-ray.)

"Oh my."

"Doc," Michael pleaded. "Just get it out!" His pain level was increasing. "I know what hell is like."

"Alright, alright. I'll be right back."

The solution to getting the fish hook out was obvious. I needed a urologist to operate. The bladder needed to be opened and the fish hook extracted surgically. The nurse informed me there was no urologist on the staff or even in the area.

"Could you please get Dr. Jansten on the phone?" I asked.

"OK." she said as she sipped her coffee. "OK."

Dr. Jansten was the chief of the clinic group that I had joined. He was now in his late sixties. He had attended medical school in the days when not much in the way of pain relief except for narcotics such as morphine could be offered to patients suffering from untreatable, incurable, or painful illnesses. In those days, most of the doctors performed their own surgery, regardless of the nature of the operation. Specialists were rare. You did it yourself. That was the standard practice.

The nurse handed me the phone. Dr. Jansten was sounding a bit inebriated. But that was nothing new. It was commonly knowledge that he drank—day and night. Regardless, he was always working. He was always in an alcoholic cloud.

"Okey Dokey. Whatcha got, Kamen?"

"Well, a male in his late twenties presents here in the ER with a fishhook in his urinary bladder and at least three inches of fishing line extending from his penis. I need a good urologist. Who do you recommend?"

"Why?"

"Why WHAT?" I asked.

"You don't need nobody. Sit tight. I'll come right down."

That sounded fine to me. Jansten did have a great deal of surgical experience. But after one hour, when he still failed to appear in the ER, I called him again.

"Dr. Jansten? Kamen here in the ER. I need for you to..."

"What's the matter with you? I told you I'm coming!"

Jansten was probably just trying to sober up a bit. But it was another thirty minutes until he appeared. Even though I had given Michael some morphine, I thought Michael would pass out from the pain, but he was hanging on. His face had a fearful grimace.

Jansten pushed open the ER doors, and without so much as a "Hello" he bellowed, "Where is he?" His frayed and unlit cigar dangled from his lips. I pointed to cubicle five. He walked over and ripped open the curtain. He did not greet or speak to Michael.

He pulled off the sheet, grabbed the penis with his left hand, and with his right hand he yanked out the fishing line with the attached hook following.

Blood spurted, stopped, then spurted again and then...drip, drip, drip, drip. Michael was beyond screaming. His mouth was wide open, and he appeared as though he wanted to scream, but he fainted. When he soon awoke, he finally mustered a high-pitched squeal. Then the retching started and the vomiting began. Then a scream. A full-blown primal scream from the depths of his body. I watched Michael, then turned to where Jansten had been standing. He was gone.

"Where's Jansten?" I asked the nurse.

"Gone."

"He left?"

"Yeah. He's gone. Left. He's not here. He's somewhere else." (I wasn't at the point of liking her yet.)

I went back to Michael and picked up the fishing line with the hook attached that was laying on the treatment tray next to the examination table. It had a strip of tissue attached to it. Was it from his urethra? Oh my God.

None of this was ever in any of the medical books I had read. I had never seen anything like this. I'd never even heard it described. As I stood there trying to think of what I was going to do next, I noticed that blood was still dripping

from Michael's penis. He'd lost at least a half cup of blood thus far. This just wasn't in the books.

My thinking was unfocused...unclear: Knock him out—no, first tell him—no, ask Dr. Jansten —give him something for pain...

I ordered a large dose of morphine.

"Are you sure about this?" asked the nurse.

"Of course I'm sure." I wasn't.

"You're giving it I.M.?" (Intra-muscularly)

"No, I.V." (Intravenous)

"You're sure about this?"

"Please! Just do it!"

She drew up the morphine. Then very slowly, I injected it into a vein. He began to relax—not totally, but some. I waited five minutes, then I injected 10 more milligrams. Finally, he fell asleep.

I called for a large diameter urethral catheter and inserted it into the bladder. The bleeding gradually subsided. The catheter was left in place for the three days he spent at the hospital. When he left, all seemed to be in perfect working order.

EPILOGUE

Michael returned to the clinic two weeks after discharge for his only post-hospitalization visit. There were no urinary troubles...excepting that the stream veered to the right and required extraordinary aim. I don't know what happened to him after that. But I can be reasonably certain that he no longer fished.

BILL BELL

The call was not entirely unexpected. I knew that Mrs. Bill Bell was angry with me when we spoke two weeks previously, but I really didn't think that she would follow through on the threat she made to me that day. But when she did, it really hurt.

"Dr. Kamen?"

Speaking."

"Dr. Kamen, this is Connie from the Lake County Medical Society."

"Yes?"

"Doctor, the Society has received a letter from the wife of one of your patients charging you with incompetence."

"From Mrs. Bill Bell, right?"

"That's right. So...uh...you already know about this?"

"Well, I suspected it anyway. This is still somewhat of a surprise, but I suppose I knew it was coming."

"Fine. Dr. Kamen, the Executive Council has its next breakfast meeting in the Gary Hotel two weeks from Sunday. I'll get a copy of her letter to your office today and if you can respond to it within a week, I'll put it on the agenda or else you can appear in person."

"No, I'll tell you what. I'll respond to it, and then if you have any questions, I can appear at the following meeting."

"Alright. Thank-you, Dr. Kamen."

A messenger arrived at my office about three hours later with a photographic copy of Mrs. Bell's communication. At first, I skimmed over it quickly, and then I went back and read it carefully— and then reread it—slowly—methodically. The facts as stated by Mrs. Bell were all there, and though they were all correct, they were nevertheless incomplete. That's because Mrs. Bell was not privy to crucial missing information.

That evening, before heading home, I took all of Mr. Bill Bell's medical records from the file so that I could spend some time at home preparing my defense. It was a tedious process because I wanted to make sure that my document was an exact account of everything that had transpired. I revised it twice in my quest for precision in this matter. When it was finished, I typed it myself and put it safely in an envelope addressed to Connie at the Medical Society. Then the next afternoon, I hand delivered my defense to Connie at the L.C.M.S. offices. I then waited for the Executive Council to meet and respond.

On Monday morning following the Executive Council's session, I received a call from Dr. Hal Simpson. Dr. Simpson had been the President of the Society for the past three years, and represented the embodiment of the conservative medical establishment— proper in bearing and demeanor—staid and sure. But this morning, he was clearly unable to control himself. He was trying to speak, but could only do so in starts and stops, punctuated by bursts of laughter. Then he'd start to cough and have to begin all over again. Finally, the conversation began in earnest.

"Jack? This is Hal. Dr. Hal Simpson."

"Yes, Hal. How are you? I expected your call, but I didn't think it would be this soon. I mean, you just met yesterday!"

"Jack...uh...Jack, I..." Laughter. Coughing. Then more laughter. "Jack, I just had to call you now. I'm telling you I've never heard of such a thing! Thanks to you, our breakfast was ruined! Everyone was laughing so hard, no one could eat. And those that had bacon and eggs already in their mouths spit it into the air and

all over the place when they heard this. I just had to call you."
More laughter. More coughing.

"Hal?"

"Yes Jack?"

"What was the decision?"

"Oh, don't worry about anything. I'll call Mrs. Bell and write her a letter explaining that there was just a lack of communication. Your treatment was..." Gurgling, laughing, coughing. "Your treatment was excellent. In fact, we all agreed it was superb."

"Well thank goodness for that. Hey, thanks a lot, Hal."

"Don't thank me. We've never had a meeting like that before. I can assure you that no one will ever forget it. By the way, did you ever make a carbon copy of your letter to us?"

"I sure did."

"Good. Keep it. You'll read it to your kids one of these days...uh...uh...when they're much older, of course."

"Of course. Well, thanks again Hal. I really appreciate it."

"I'll be talking to you, Jack."

Just about a year ago, I came across that letter as I was packing for our move from Gary to our current home in Indianapolis. It pretty much tells the whole story.

Dr. Hal Simpson

President, Lake County Medical Society

Chairman of the Executive Council

1125 North Broadway

Gary, 6, Indiana
138

Dear Dr. Simpson,

I feel that the best way to respond to Mrs. Bell's charge of incompetency would be to tell you and the council exactly what happened relating to the incident in question. You can then be the judge.

Mr. Bill "Bull" Bell came into my office on February 20 complaining of a penile discharge that he stated he noted only that morning. A smear, which I did in the office, verified his worse suspicions, as it displayed gram positive for cocci.

When I told him that he had gonorrhea, he turned sweaty and ash white. His mouth stood agape and he said nothing.

Immediately, I tried to assure him that he really had nothing to worry about; that penicillin would cure it, and that he would be left with no after effects. My arguments didn't help to ease his agitation. He remained completely unresponsive and simply stared blankly at me.

Finally, I asked him what was wrong; what was bothering him so. He then started with the usual litany that I'm certain I heard at least a hundred different times. He said that despite his nickname, he never before cheated on his wife...except for three days before he came in, and even then it was just once; and it happened because he had been out with the boys and they'd all had a few beers and all ended up in the whore house across the street.

I said nothing as he spoke. I just listened...until he came to his real problem.

He told me that he had "intercoursed" with his wife last night and did I think she had it too.

I know you are well aware that a patient with an obvious discharge has had the urethritis for at least two days previously.

I therefore was compelled to tell him that there was indeed a strong likelihood that she too had contracted the disease.

Terror suddenly filled his face. He told me that his wife would kill him. What was he going to do? Was there any way I could help him?

I thought about the situation for a few minutes, and then developed my reasoning. Here was a couple, more or less happily married for fourteen years with three children. Why not bend the rules just a little bit? What harm would a small lie do if the marriage and family could be saved? His wife and children are also patients of mine. I knew them all quite well, and knowing her, she may well have killed him.

I told him I wanted to examine his mouth, despite his protestations that he "never did anything like that". He finally consented to the examination. I looked at the tongue and mucous membranes very carefully. Then I sat down with him to explain everything.

"Now Bill," I told him, "There just may be a chance, although a small chance, that you may have a mild case of trench mouth. Now I'm not saying that you have trench mouth, but there's always a possibility."

He looked somewhat bewildered. I assured him that trench mouth was NOT a venereal disease. I then told him that trench mouth responds quite well to tetracycline capsules which also is very effective against gonorrhea. I explained that if he also kissed his wife last night, that she too could possibly "catch" trench mouth and that both of them should take the tetracycline.

He understood my plan perfectly. His face brightened and he readily agreed to it. He would get the capsules and give it to his wife and his worries would be over.

I thought the incident would be over too, but three days later, I received a phone call from Mrs. Bell. She was understandably quite angry.

Essentially, she said that she awoke that morning with the most awful vaginal discharge and dysuria (painful urination). She tried to contact me but I was busy in surgery. She decided therefore to see Dr. Woodward, who, as you know, is an OB/GYN in Hammond. He promptly told her what she had.

She confronted her husband when he returned home and told him that he must have gonorrhea too because she certainly had no other contact. She wanted to know why he didn't see me about the condition.

This is where the trouble lies. He told her that he indeed DID see me about the discharge he was having, but that I told him it was trench mouth. "Well," she said, "Dr. Kamen, if you don't know the difference between gonorrhea and trench mouth, you don't deserve to be a doctor! I'm reporting you!!!"

The above outlines the gist of what happened. I leave judgement to you and the council.

Sincerely, Jack M. Kamen, M.D.

EPILOGUE

Mrs. Bill Bell neither killed nor left her husband. He and the children continued as my patients. However, I never saw Mrs. Bell again. And for many years afterward, the standard greeting of a former council member to me was, "Well, Jack, do you know the difference between gonorrhea and trench mouth yet?"

SELMA

This one really had me puzzled. First of all, it was totally unexpected. I mean, why should I have anticipated it any more than I would have expected Gary, Indiana to be hit by a major earthquake? It just didn't make much sense. Here we were, Shirley and I, married to each other for the past fifteen years and, like most married couples, we had our share of marital spats. So what was going on here?

When I walked through the door that evening, I could immediately sense that something was different. Our four kids came running excitedly to greet me, as they did each evening. They jumped on by back, grabbed on to my legs, and shouted a chorus of, "Daddy! Daddy! Daddy's home! Mommy, Daddy's home!!" I had talked to Shirley not thirty minutes ago, as I was leaving the hospital. Everything seemed fine. But this evening, Shirley didn't come to the door with the children. That was unusual. She also didn't answer when I called her name.

"Sher?" No answer.

"Shirley?" Silence.

"Shirley, I'm home!" Still, not a sound. I hobbled into the kitchen with the children still hanging on me, looking for Shirley. She was standing at the stove, stirring chicken soup...and crying. For the most part, her tears flowed silently, but soon, she started sobbing.

"Sher! Shirley...what's wrong?"

Silence.

"Is your mother alright?" She had recently fractured her arm.

"Fine!" came Shirley's terse reply.

"Sher—come on now. Tell me what's wrong! Are you OK?"

Silence.

"Oh Sher...it's you. You're sick. Oh my gosh...what happened?"

"Nothing happened and I'm not sick and no one is sick except maybe you're sick...I'm the last one you asked about, if I was sick...but that doesn't matter, because I really don't give a damn."

It became clear that a "hello" kiss at this point was not on the menu. I stood there in silence. I didn't have a clue about what was going on...what's more, I had never in our entire married lives heard Shirley use anything that even came close to a curse word. For her to use the word "damn" at all, much less when the children were present, immediately signaled something was terribly, terribly wrong.

"For crying out loud, Sher...for crying out loud...what happened? Just give me a little hint. What happened?"

The silent treatment was gaining momentum again.

"Just a hint, Sher, is all I want. Just a hint."

The chicken soup, by this time, had to be dizzy as she angrily jerked the spoon through the pot. As the silence continued, I played out in my mind the phone conversation Shirley and I had a half-hour earlier, and even reviewed the events of the past few days. There was nothing unusual that I could recall, except perhaps that the office ran late a couple of evenings, but even that wasn't all that rare...so that left nothing...absolutely nothing! This was the darnedest thing. Finally, she turned to me and spoke.

"You've got a house call. Selma Hoskins called because she said her baby is sick. She wants you to come over."

I glanced over at the telephone message pad. Selma Hoskins' name, phone number and address were neatly written on the page. I picked up the phone and dialed. The situation didn't sound urgent, so I told her I'd come around in the morning. I hung up the phone and looked over towards Shirley. She turned to tell our eldest daughter to tell me that dinner was almost ready. This was getting serious. Clearly, she didn't want to speak to me.

And that's the way things were throughout dinner. She would communicate with me only through the children, who were delighted with this new game.

"Suzy, tell your father that I cancelled our dinner date with the Bresler's this Saturday."

"Uh, Dad, Mom says that you guys aren't going out on Saturday night."

"Thank-you, Suzy."

"What else, Mom? What else can I tell Daddy?"

"Nothing, Suzy, thank-you."

"Daddy, do you have anything you want me to tell Mommy?"

"No, thank-you, Suzy."

"Can we play too?" asked our two youngest, David and Daniel.

I wasn't enjoying this, but apparently, the game wasn't going to end at dinner. That night, Shirley slept on the couch, and for the first time in our entire married lives, she didn't get up at 5:00 a.m. the next morning to make me my breakfast. I went to the local diner as confused as I had ever been.

At work that day, I was depressed, dejected and puzzled, wondering what in the world I could have done to cause Shirley to be so angry. How had I sinned? What in the heck did I do?

When I came home that evening, I was expecting more of the same...and I got it. More crying...speaking to me only through the children.

144

"Mommy's crying forever, Daddy." volunteered our youngest son, Daniel. I could see that. Her eyes were very swollen and red. But by the time dinner was ready to be served, she had regained her composure and served the meal— perfunctorily and mechanically. Then:

"Did you make that housecall on Missus Selma Hoskins?"

Aha! At last! A clue! Shirley had never before asked me about a housecall. Wait a minute...could it be...Missus Selma Hoskins? Why the emphasis on Missus? What could she possibly...

"It is Missus Hoskins, isn't it Jack? She does have a husband, doesn't she Jack? And her husband lives with her, isn't that right Jack?"

"Yes, yes and yes. But I'm beginning to understand now. Something about Selma Hoskins has you bugged, right? That's what it is! What's bugging you about Mrs. Hoskins? That's it, isn't it?"

Her pent up rage came bursting out in a torrent of fury.

"Don't play the innocent with me. I know what's going on here! I know everything! Down to every last little detail! I know what's been going on between you two, so you can't deny it, because I know everything!"

I was absolutely dumbstruck. I sat there frozen—totally immobile—and her rantings continued.

"I should have seen this earlier! How could you do this to me! How! What have I ever done to deserve this from you! How could you do such a thing?!!"

Stop the presses. Me and Selma Hoskins? Shirley thinks that Selma Hoskins and I are...are...uh...? Aw, come on. No way. This was unbelievable. Finally, Shirley stopped, and then the crying began again wildly.

145

"Sher...Sher...I swear on my life, on the kids, on everything we have that I have never had anything to do with another woman...ever! Please believe me Sher! This is madness...utter madness! I swear by everything, Shirley! I swear!"

We both looked up and suddenly realized that the children had heard everything and were crying. Suzy was almost uncontrollable. We did our best to console them and even laughed and tried to convince them that they had seen a "grown-up" game. We finally managed to convince them to finish their dinner. Then we sent them down to the basement to watch TV. By that time, both Shirley and I were calmer. We went into the living room and faced each other, and for the first time in a day and a half, spoke openly with each other.

"Sher...just tell me what happened that would make you even think such a thing. I want you to start at the very beginning."

Shirley hesitated only slightly. Then she began her story, and when she had finished, I laughed so hard and so long that the children came bounding up the stairs to see what was going on. (Maybe another "grown-up" game?) They didn't want to miss anything that was this good. But in order for me to explain to Shirley what she had obviously grossly misunderstood, I had to threaten to take away dessert privileges from the kids before they would retreat back to the basement. I took Shirley's hand.

"Sher, you know I love you and only you. Now, let me tell you the whole story, and after I've finished, if you think I've been unfaithful, you could do with me what you wish. But I ask only one thing. Don't say or do anything until I've finished. OK?"

She looked at me tearfully and nodded. I began.

The whole thing started about four years ago, about one year after I began work at the Indiana Harbor Clinic. Father Michael, a Catholic Priest of the Lady of Guadalupe Parish, called and asked

if he could come into the office to discuss a "very delicate matter."
I had met Father Michael several months earlier when he
recruited me to become the physician at the local orphan home.
Because Father Michael appeared to be quite agitated, I agreed to
meet with him later that same evening after I had seen my last
patient.

Father Michael was a priest in his early thirties, and, as I was to
learn later, a convert to Catholicism. (I asked about his previous
religion but he refused to answer.) He was a model priest, active
in all community affairs, and a pioneer in battling the burgeoning
drug culture. But now, as he entered my office he looked every
inch a defeated man.

"Jack," he began. "I've got a real problem."

"Sit down, Padre."

He sat down in the chair next to my desk. He nervously fumbled
with some paper clips on my desk.

"Before I begin, Jack, I think I need to explain something to you
about Catholic practice. I don't think Jews do the same thing."

"Jews don't do the same thing? In what?"

"In marriage."

"Well, Jewish couples frequently meet with the Rabbi before they
marry and mixed marriages are frowned upon and..."

"No, no, no. It's nothing like that." he interrupted. "It's just that
what we do isn't really voluntary. Couples have to attend what we
call Pre-Cana conferences."

I had not heard of this.

"What we do is essentially discuss the duties and obligations of
the marriage partners to each other and to the church."

"That doesn't sound like too much of a problem."

"Well, Jack, it's a little more complicated than that." He shifted nervously in his chair, adjusted his collar, tugged on the sleeve of his jacket, and ran his hand through his hair.

"You see," he began again. "There are two parts to the Conferences. There's the spiritual part, and then there's the...the..the...uh...what we call the corporeal or the...uh...I'd guess you'd call it the...uh...shall we say the...uh... physical part."

Having finally said it, there was a look of utter relief and he started to relax. Now I was beginning to see and understand Father Michael's problem.

"Padre, you feel somewhat uncomfortable teaching the physical...I mean the corporeal part?"

"Yeah, that's it. That's it. I just can't do it, Jack. I tried, but I can't do it. But you're Jewish, Jack. You can do it."

Suddenly, his face turned bright red.

"No, no, Jack. That isn't really what I meant. I meant that not being Catholic you can teach it scientifically and dispassionately...I mean without having to think or say anything about Catholic dogma. It's not that you're Jewish, it's just that you're not Catholic."

"Father Michael, I understand completely. Don't worry. I'll do it. Just tell me what it involves and if you have teaching materials and where it's held."

"All of that will be up to you, Jack. Everything. As a rule, you meet first with the men, and then with the women, and then both together. I have some booklets and a few anatomy charts, but they're almost useless. You can start from scratch...whatever you want to do, do it. And, uh, of course, you know we can't pay for it, Jack."

"Of course." I was already the examining physician for the local Catholic charities, and I was the nuns' physician in the catechism school, so this was going to be another "out-of-my-faith" duty. It sounded like it was going to be pretty interesting, and having never done anything like it before, it was going to be a learning experience for me too. (Boy, would it ever!)

"We have eight couples at present waiting to be married." said Father Michael. "I'm already doing my part. When can you start yours, Jack?"

"Give me about a week to prepare. We can probably meet every Wednesday night at 9:00 in my office. We'll start with the men."

I rapidly worked to prepare for the first session. I read as much material on sex education as I could. I found several wall charts on the male and female anatomy from the recently closed hospital school of nursing. These would be helpful. Soon, it was Wednesday. At 9:00 sharp, all eight men showed up and managed to cram into my small office. When everyone was settled, I introduced myself, had my "students" do the same, and then it was time to begin. What happened next is a matter of opinion. To me, it was a disaster, but to the prospective grooms, well...

The grooms-to-be were not much more than boys. They were, for the most part, of first generation Spanish descent. There were only two others, a Slav and a Pole who were not. But they were all macho men; all-knowing, all-wise and in my office for the brief "how-to's" only because they had to be there before there could be any "I do's." Soon after the "lecture" began, there were smirks and asides between the men. I wanted to cancel the class and tell them all to leave. I didn't need the grief. I persisted. Something inside me told me to at least give it one more try. And so I did.

I began with an explanation of the course goals. I told them I would answer any questions or problems they would have. "We could teach you a few things, Doc!" We were underway.

Using the cutaway chart of the male anatomy, I tried to teach them the anatomy and physiology of their bodies.

"I don't look like that inside! I'm a lot..you know...neater!"

"Doc...erection. Uh, does that mean hard-on?"

"I don't need no artery or vein to get that big. All I need is women!"

Laughter. Heckling. More snickering. Awful.

Next, I pulled down the frontal chart showing the male genitalia. There was a short pause. Then a barrage of reactions.

"That guy ain't hung at all."

"His wife is gonna be damn disappointed."

"This guy can't be for real!"

Oddly enough, their comments about the chart figure's lack of endowment were valid. Remember, these charts were teaching tools for student nurses, and not centerfolds from "Playgirl."

The male anatomy portion of the class was finished in about thirty minutes. We had a small recess, and everyone went to get a cup of coffee. I told them to return in five minutes, but most were back before then, eager to proceed with the study of female anatomy.

I began the review of the female anatomy as I had begun the study of the male. First, I discussed the physiology and internal anatomy. Development, hormones, menstruation, ovulation, implantation, and fetal development were explored. As the lecture proceeded, I noticed that their attentiveness was waning. Then I pulled down the full frontal female anatomy chart. Near pandemonium.

"Now SHE'S built. But my Rosa's bigger!"

"I changed my mind! The wedding's off! I want HER instead!!!"

"Now you're cookin' Doc! You got her phone number?"

I tried to salvage the discussion by continuing with cold scientific language.

"Now this, as you know, is a mammary gland," I said.

Pandemonium.

"That's no 'mammy' gland, that's a boob. That's one for Borden's dairy!"

I continued. "Now this is the mons pubis that..."

Bedlam.

"You mean the man's pubis is where the man goes. We already know that!"

"Jose', you're gross," said one groom. "Do you know that? You're gross. The Doc here is trying to teach you something. Now shut-up."

An ally?

I muddled through the rest of the female anatomy discussion. I hesitated to show the last chart. I debated it for some time. I felt like Father Michael. I just didn't want to do this anymore. Finally I decided to show it. Things couldn't possibly get any worse.

I pulled the chart down. And there it was; a larger than life illustration of the female perineum from the front with the legs apart.

Total silence. Then...

"That's pretty ugly...ain't it?"

"No way, that's not really what it looks like."

"Aw, how th' hell would you know what it really looks like? Or did Rosa show you?"

A short-lived, playful scuffle quickly ensued between the two, but was soon quelled by the noncombatants. Celibacy and virginity, at least in concept, were still the standard. When it was brought into question, it was a no-go, even for a man. But the room was now under control, and the lecture proceeded.

"Alright. Now that we now know how men and women are built and what happens in their bodies, we're going to discuss the sex act itself."

At first, silence. Then...

"Come on, you're no expert. You want an expert? I'm an expert."

Another scuffle ensued, this time longer than the first. Tension was building.

"OK, OK, then we can just skip this part." I said.

"No! No! Go on! Go on! I'll keep 'em quiet."

"Alright. The first thing we'll discuss is how not to make love."

"That's rich. That's rich."

"Will you shaddup and let the Doc talk?"

"How not to make love," I continued. "is that you don't just jump into bed, penetrate her, and smoke a cigarette."

"Uh Doc," said one of the students. "What do you mean 'perpetrate' her?"

"No, not 'perpetrate.' Penetrate." I said. "That means to enter her...to put your penis into her."

"Oh! You mean screw her, right?"

"Well yes," I said. "What you just said...that's what I mean."

"Well then, I don't get it. I mean, if you're not gonna 'perpetrate' her then what th' hell else you gonna do with her? I mean, that's why we're gettin' married for crissake. I want to 'perpetrate' her legally!"

"No, no. That's not what I mean. You've got to let me finish. I mean that you have to prepare her, and yourself, for the actual sex act."

"Oh, is that when you give each other a bath?" asked one student.

"No, you dumbhead," said another. "He means you've got to ask her first."

"Please. Let me finish," I said. "What I mean is that you must prepare each other sexually. You must arouse and excite each other as much as you can before the actual sex act takes place."

"Hell, that's easy! All she has to do is look, or even feel and she knows, she knows."

"What, you're already teaching Rosa?" someone asked.

No scuffle this time. Just glares. I continued.

"No, that isn't what I mean either. What I'm talking about is arousing each other by gently fondling, caressing, touching, whispering, or kissing each other...exciting each other's erotic zones."

Silence. Finally:

"Uh...what are 'exotic' zones?"

"Not 'exotic'...erotic. Those are the places that...uh...turns a person on when you stroke them or kiss them there. The male has only one or two erotic zones, but a woman ordinarily has about ten."

"Ten? A woman has ten? I only know three...you know...two on top and one on the bottom."

"Maybe Rosa didn't tell you about the others."

Another scuffle. Now I had their attention. Most had their eyes fixed on the perineum chart. I went on to explain how a woman could be stimulated by stroking or gently blowing into her ear; how one should start by caressing the sides of the breasts, instead of just reaching for the breasts themselves. I told them how to gently touch the sides of the hips first, and then work their way to the inner thighs, and then the various parts of the vulva and finally the clitoris, and then...

The class was now squirming. Most were adjusting their crotches. No one spoke. After I'd finished, I called for questions. At first, the silence persisted...but it was short-lived.

"Uh, do all girls got these things?"

"You mean erotic zones?"

"Yeah, that's them."

"Well, yes. But depending on their culture or how they were raised, women respond differently with varying degrees of excitement or arousal. We know, for example, that a prostitute may not have as many recognizable erotic zones, but a woman who has been pampered and even sheltered all her life may have even more than ten."

"Hey, man, your Rosa's got none or she's got twenty. But I think it's twenty. That's why she looks like she's always got the hots."

"OK, that's it!" said Rosa's intended. "I'm gonna kill you..." "Let's calm down now everyone." I said. "We're all just a little uptight right now." Suddenly, the room filled with laughter.

"You two shake hands." I insisted. "Come on...shake hands."

154

The two men got up and did as I said. More questions soon followed...first in dribbles, then in torrents.

"Can you go over the erotic zone part again, Doc?" (I did.)

"Can you give this talk to us again?" (I'm booked. Sorry.)

"Can I come again to a new class?" (Sure.)

At eleven o'clock, the class was over.

The next week, I was expecting the eight men's fiancees. But curiously, fifteen women showed up. My office could not accommodate all of them, so I took the class into the waiting room. The women's class was similar to the men's class the week before. I introduced myself and had the women do the same. I went through the male and female anatomy charts, and then proceeded with the discussion on sex. The questions they had following the talk were predictable.

"Did you tell all of this to our guys?"

"Did they already know all of this?"

"Do they really know how we feel?"

"Do they know what they should do on our first night?"

Nervous laughter permeated the question and answer session. The evening went well, but it was the class with both the men and the women that I had to face the next week. I certainly didn't anticipate what happened.

At 9:00 sharp, approximately thirty people were in my waiting room. I knew that the session could not be taught with that many people. I had to insist that only the original eight couples stay for the class with the promise that I would teach an extra session during the next cycle of classes.

The session lasted two hours. Their frank questions initiated discussion, but that still seemed unable to satiate their interest.

"Can we come back if we need a booster?" (Yes.)

"Can you tell him what he's doing wrong?"(Much laughter) "No! I mean if he does it wrong?" (More laughter.)

"Do our folks know about these things?" (I'm not sure.)

No question about it. The class was a true success. Three days after the final session, I received a call from Father Michael.

"Jack, what in heaven's name are you doing? My phone is always ringing! So many people say they want to convert! But I'm finding out that what they really want is your class! What's going on, Jack?"

"I'm just doing what you asked me to do."

"You're sure?"

"Don't worry Padre. Everything's kosher."

"Alright. Thanks Jack."

My classes continued to grow in size and soon they began to interfere with my practice. I couldn't begin my normal round of house calls until eleven or twelve o'clock on Wednesday nights. Finally, I had to cut the classes down to one complete cycle every three months.

It was during one of these sessions that Selma Hoskins appeared with her husband. She was a rather unattractive, plump, and slightly dowdy looking woman in her mid-twenties. She appeared to have suffered the boring vicissitudes of the wife of a steel mill worker in a steel town that offered a quality of life that offered a poor quality of life. Day to day, her existence was one of trudging drudgery.

156

Selma, having been to see me in my office a couple of times for her baby, convinced Father Michael to let her and her husband come to my "sex" class that she had heard so much about from her friends and neighbors. Despite the fact that she had been married for several years, Selma told Father Michael that both she and her husband could use a refresher course to give their marriage a boost. Father Michael reluctantly agreed. He was uncomfortable with the fact that the "sex" class had gained such notoriety in the community, and that everyone knew it was being held under his supervision. But there was also a positive side to its popularity. Father Michael was able to spread his gospel to a larger flock. The class was the bait that lured them "home."

Selma was very attentive in class. She always came with a pad of paper and a pen so she could take notes. As I proceeded, she would also write down questions that she would ask me after the lecture was over.

By the time the final session ended, Selma came in looking better than I'd ever seen her. She was brighter...smiling; and even wore makeup and a hint of perfume. I'd never known her to do either. She and her husband sat holding hands the entire time...often whispering to each other during the evening. When they left, she thanked me and told me what a wonderful difference the class had made in their lives. Even when she came into the office a few weeks later for her baby's appointment, she still seemed to be elated. During that office visit, she thanked me again.

And so, I told Shirley, that's it...the entire story. There was nothing more to tell.

"And that, Sher, is why you got that phone call."

Shirley sat there looking greatly relieved. She sighed deeply.

"Look, Jack, how would you have felt if you were in my place and received a phone call like that? Imagine picking up the phone and hearing, "Hello, this is Selma Hoskins. Is this Mrs. Kamen?" "Yes." "Mrs. Kamen could you have Dr. Kamen come over to my house to see my baby? He has a fever and diarrhea. I'll give you my address and phone number." She did and then she said, "Mrs. Kamen, you must be very happy." I told her I was, and then she said, "Dr. Kamen must make you verr-r-ry happy." I said , "He does." And then...then she said, "Oh, he knows everything there is to know about sex. He knows everything. Everything! And he taught me everything. He's made me so happy!" Jack, I just stood there holding the receiver. I couldn't move or talk. I couldn't do anything. I don't even know what I said to her after that. I think I just said, "Alright" and hung up. Oh Yankel, thank-God I know now what happened. Thank God!"

Shirley and I made up that night.

EPILOGUE

The next time I had to make a house call at Selma Hoskins', I took Shirley along. She went up to the apartment with me, chatted with Selma and even held the baby. On our way out, we met Selma's husband coming up the stairs.

"Dr. Kamen! Hello!" he said, and then nodded to Shirley. "Did Selma tell you? She's going to have another baby!"

"No, she didn't! That's wonderful!"

"It sure was, Doc. And...uh...thanks again for...uh...uh..."

"That's alright. It was my pleasure."

Shirley glanced over at me. But she was still smiling.

LITTLE PETER, GEORGE, AND LITTLE STAMOS

The Greek community of Indiana Harbor was very closely knit. Though they only numbered about 400 families, they became quite a force in the community: politically and financially...much more so than their numbers would indicate. No member of the community was unknown to another, and even though there were two Greek Orthodox Churches in the area, there did not seem to be any internecine rivalries.

Any event of any significance that happened to any member of the group involved the entire community. This can be borne out in the telling of several incidents that I had personally witnessed...the last of which is perhaps unique in the annals of medicine.

(It's important to note here that I had seen no Greek patients during the first year and a half of my practice. There were two competent Greek physicians in town. They knew the language, which enabled them to establish a rapport with not only the "new" immigrants, but also with their children and even their grandchildren. The latter two groups were taught Greek in the churches' catechism schools. These doctors were helpful in their community.)

It was with some surprise then that I saw Mrs. Anastasia Kovourinas come into the waiting room with her five year old son, Peter. She and her husband were part owners, along with another Greek family, of a popular eatery across the street from my office. It seemed that most of the family members worked in the restaurant, as was true for most of the other Greek-owned restaurants in town.

"Doctor," she began as she came into the office. "I've been everywhere. I even saw a big skin doctor in Chicago for three months. Seventy-five dollars for every visit! Imagine, Doctor.

Every week they tell me use this salve, use that salve, this medicine, that medicine, this bath, that bath...and nothing, Doctor! Nothing! If anything, worse...a lot worse. You are the eighth or maybe even the ninth doctor. But you're a Jew. And I know, Jews can help."

I was to learn later that there was an empathy between the Greeks and the Jews...much different than some apparent ingrained hostilities between other ethnic groups.

Mrs. Kovourivas peeled off Peter's shirt and pulled down his trousers and shorts. Poor little Peter was covered with infected and scabbed sores over his entire body. He scratched incessantly at them, causing them to weep a yellow serous discharge. The areas surrounding each pustule was reddened and obviously infected.

"How long has he been like this?" I asked her.

"About nine months. And all this time, he's been getting worse."

"Now exactly what have you done for it?"

"What have I done? What haven't I done? Look!"

With that, she emptied a large paper bag. Out came at least twenty different ointments, salves, and lotions. The names of the Greek doctors were on some of the prescription labels, and there were also some with the name of a prominent Chicago dermatologist.

"Mrs. Kovourivas," I said. "He'll be well in three or four days." I even surprised myself, because I had never promised anything like that before. I was always overly cautious, allowing at least a small escape hatch. But I knew what Little Peter had. I was sure of it. As an intern at Cook County Hospital, I had seen this repeatedly at the outpatient clinic. The old Viennese-born dermatologist who was our professor taught me exactly how to treat it. What Little Peter had was endemic in the poorer of Indian Harbor. Perhaps that is why the high-priced dermatologist had missed it.

"Mrs. K., Peter has scabies, and it's possible to get rid of it." Scabies is a skin condition caused by a small parasite that burrows and takes up residence under the skin. It is usually found in areas where hygiene is poor, and is communicable. I was sure that the latter accounted for poor Peter's unfortunate condition. He had probably contracted it from a schoolmate.

The diagnosis was easily confirmed by carefully shaving off a lesion, and after simple preparation with an alkali solution, looking at it with a microscope.

I invited Mrs. K. to peek into the microscope lens so that she could see the parasite that was the cause of her son's condition. For a long while, she just stood there looking horrified.

"You mean this...this ANIMAL has been living on my little boy? Do you mean to tell me that he has a hundred...maybe a thousand of these worms all over him? And you mean that no one else..."

"Now look, Anastasia, I told you we'd get rid of them and we will! I'm sure."

I took my prescription pad and wrote out an order for an ointment comprised of crude sulfur and crude lanolin. Luckily, pharmacists were still compounding prescriptions at that time. The finished concoction would be quite thick, gooey, and messy.

I gave Anastasia the prescription sheet and I explained that she must first bathe little Peter, and then apply the mixture all over his entire body. The next morning, she was to wash off the ointment, and repeat the process each night for three nights.

It wasn't surprising that she looked hesitant and doubtful.

"Look," I said, "If it works, you make me some Baklava. If not, there's no charge. Do we have a deal?" She smiled.

In two weeks, Anastasia returned carrying a large tin filled to the top with homemade Baklava.

"I can't believe it! I can't! Everything is gone...everything! There isn't one sore left! We are going to feed you in the restaurant for a whole year! A whole year...free for you!!"

After little Peter was cured of his scabies, I suddenly experienced a trickle and then a constant flow of new Greek patients. The language barrier didn't present too much of a problem because the non-English speaking patients always brought their own interpreters with them.

The numbers of Greek patients I was treating continued to grow until two years later, when I received an urgent request to pay a house call on a rather well-to-do elder of the church. Though he was only forty-five years old, he attained marked success in the burgeoning fast food industry. I had known him since he opened his first "Quick George" hamburger stand. It wasn't long before he owned twenty others just like it throughout Northwest Indiana. I left my office patients and was at his home in about five minutes.

It was clear to me at first glance that "Quick George" himself was near death. He was gasping for air, fighting for breath. His face was ashen...it had already taken on a death-white tone. His skin was cold and dripping with sweat. He had the look of terror when death is imminent.

At that time, (in the fifties), ambulance services were a farce. In an emergency, a squad was usually dispatched from the nearest fire department, which had no life-saving equipment except for oxygen tanks. Often, an ambulance from a local funeral home was summoned, but often, their drivers may have been busy with "paying customers",and if they did come, it was always at their leisure. (They weren't used to working at a fast pace.)

There were several men around George's bedside. I motioned for them to join me in the other room.

"Look," I said. "I think George has had a massive heart attack. He's got to get to the hospital immediately. I'll need you to help me get him into my car."

Together, we lifted him into the back seat and, with his brother and his good friend, raced to the hospital. Four or five minutes later, we reached the emergency room. But it was too late. As we began to lift him from the car, I could see he was dead. This was in the days before CPR.

In the couple of days following George's death, Greek patients who had scheduled appointments with me cancelled them. And during the next few weeks and months, the number of Greek patients I saw rapidly dwindled. I'd heard "through the grapevine" that it wasn't that they considered George's death to be my fault, it was just that he'd died in my car, and that was a bad omen. After a short time, I just considered my Greek practice to be finished. There was nothing I could do. So it came as somewhat of a surprise when I picked up the chart of a patient who had scheduled an appointment with me about six months later. "Christina Kostetiopoulous," I called.

This should be interesting...as she followed me into my office.

Christina was the oldest daughter of Zarfia and Theos Kostetiopoulous. Her family owned a profitable trucking company in Michigan City, Indiana. Though I had never had her as a patient, I had treated members of her family. She entered the office and said hello. I could see that she was deeply disturbed.

"Hi Chris. How are you?"

"Dr. Kamen, I'm getting married next month...in fact my wedding is in three weeks. Uh...you and your wife are welcome to come if you're free."

She then burst into a staccato of sobbing. She covered her face with her handkerchief, but her tears fell between her open fingers and onto the floor.

"Chris..Chris...what's wrong?"

No response. Her crying became more and more profuse.

"Chris...Chris. Chris!" I gently asked. "How far along are you?"

Suddenly, her crying eased. Slowly, she removed her hands from her face. I sat there silently as she took a tissue from her purse and dabbed at her eyes. Finally.

"About two months."

"Alright Chris, sit down. Now how many periods have you missed?"

"Two."

I calculated her expected delivery date.

"What am I going to do, Dr. Kamen? What am I going to do? I want to die. I just want to die. My mother is going to die. And I really want to die too! I do! I do! " More sobbing. Harder and harder.

"Now wait Chris. Is the baby by the same man you're going to marry?"

Mistake. I ought not to have asked her that question. Not being a virgin and conceiving out of wedlock were two of the ultimate disgraces that could befall a Greek girl. But to imply that she was "loose" too made her unbearable situation more unendurable than before. I had to backtrack.

"Look Chris, I had to ask you that from a medical point of view. You know, blood types and things like that. I know you and I know your family. I knew the answer before I even asked. I'm sorry."

Chris appeared to accept my explanation. She nodded, but then assumed a desperate expression.

"Look Chris, I have an answer to this."

Her eyes suddenly widened.

"No Dr. Kamen! No! We don't want an abortion!"

"Chris, first of all, you know that abortions are illegal, and besides, I'm also dead set against it. But I have a different idea. I want you to just stop worrying. Don't say anything to anyone, Chris. Not to anyone. Do you understand? And come back in a couple of days, and then I'll tell you what we'll do. Trust me. And don't worry."

Now I was in this thing deep. I had no definite plan, but I did have a scheme formulating in my mind as I sat looking at the desperate Chris. At first, my plan was disconnected and I needed time to organize it. I had to make the plan clear to myself. Then I had to consult with medical allies at the hospital. Two days. That should be enough time, I thought.

That night, I thought about nothing but my plan for Chris. Finally, I decided exactly what I was going to do. Yes, I thought. This should work. This should definitely work. It all fell into place.

The next morning, I went straight to the administrator's office. Sister Cordelia was an "all-business" kind of administrator, but always seemed to retain the gentleness and understanding of her vocation. I outlined the problem for her and the solution I had concocted. Her decision was prompt.

"If you can get the approval of Sister Welsa (the supervisor of obstetrics and newborn nursery), I'll approve it."

"A deal."

I ran up the four floors to the OB ward and found Sister Welsa at the chart desk.

"Sister, can I speak with you in private for a moment?"

She glared at me.

"If this is another one of your crazy, nutty schemes, then I want absolutely nothing to do with it. And I mean it!"

"Sister, please. Just hear me out. Sister Cordelia has already approved it." (A small lie was justified.) "But I wanted to get your OK before going ahead with it."

"I said no, Dr. Kamen, and I mean no!!!" she said emphatically, her face reddening. "But you can tell me what you were thinking anyway...even though it won't make any difference."

I told her of my plan, just as I had outlined it to Sister Cordelia. Then I waited. There was a protracted pause.

"Look, Sister, " I said, shattering the uneasy silence. "Her life may actually depend on this. Truly. Listen, you certainly don't want her to go to some back alley place and have an abortion, do you?" Abortion. I knew the mention of the word would work. Another pause. Then...

"Now look, Dr. Kamen, of all the lunatics, you're the worst. But I'm going to allow you to do it...don't ask me why, but I'll do it...only because of the baby, and definitely not because of you. It's not you. Do you understand? Not you!!!!!"

"Oh yes, I understand Sister! I understand!" This was incredible. "Oh, and Sister...bless you!"

"Sure. But if anything goes wrong, it's going to be your...uh...end!"

"Sister!"

166

"Uh, you're sure Sister Cordelia approved it?"

"Would I ever, ever lie to you Sister?"

"I wouldn't answer that." Good.

With my plan in place, I went back to the office to call Chris. I told her what was going to take place, and that the whole thing had been approved by the administration. The next day, she came into the office with her fiancee as I had asked. Together, we went through all the details again. I had to be sure that they understood exactly how the plan would work. They smiled and nodded and held hands as we talked. This was really going to work, I thought. For both their sakes, and for the baby's. It had to. They were ecstatic when they left the office.

Shirley and I received an invitation to their wedding. It was the first time either of us had ever witnessed a wedding in a Greek Orthodox church. We went and were both mesmerized. It was quite moving and very beautiful. Chris was lovely and radiant as she proceeded down the aisle, and Adonis, her fiancee, couldn't seem to keep his eyes off his beautiful bride.

So far, so good.

Six months later, about the time I was expecting word from Chris, I got a phone call from her mother at about ten o'clock one evening.

"Doctor, doctor! It's Christina! She's hurting bad! You know they are here living with us and I think she's going to lose her baby Doctor! She's not due for another three or four months Doctor! She told me to call you right away! What should we do Dr. Kamen?"

"Alright, now listen. It sounds to me like she's gone into premature labor. Get her to the hospital as quickly as you can, and I'll meet you there."

"Doctor, is she going to lose the baby?"

"Don't worry. We'll do everything we can. Just get her to the hospital now!"

When I examined Chris in the ER, she was almost fully dilated. We rushed her up to OB, and in less than one hour, little Stamos was born weighing 6 lbs, 2 oz. He was beautiful and with a lusty cry. The plan was now officially underway.

The nurses in the newborn nursery had been alerted and briefed by both me and Sister Welsa. I wrapped the baby and carried him into the nursery myself.

"This is the one, isn't it?" asked Mrs. Selman, the charge nurse.

"Yes. Now you know what to do?"

"Yes. He goes into the isolation unit with absolutely no visitors. What's the birthweight?"

"Make it two pounds, one ounce. And don't forget Mrs. Selman...no visitors!!!"

"Right, Doctor."

I went into the waiting room. Adonis was there along with both sets of anxious grandparents. They quickly crowded around me, eager for news about Chris and the baby. Adonis gave me a glance, but pressed me for information along with the others. Good. He was playing his part.

"Now look," I began. "We tried to stop her labor, but she had just progressed too far, and we couldn't. Chris is doing just fine, and the baby...it's a boy...is doing OK too. But as you know, the baby is very premature, and he weighs just one ounce over two pounds. I had to isolate the baby in a special incubator for premies so he can't catch any germs. So I'm sorry, I just can't allow any visitors whatsoever..no one...not even you, Adonis. And we certainly can't

168

take him to be displayed in the nursery. That would be too risky right now. I'm not willing to take that chance, and I'm sure you're not either."

"Oh doctor, doctor!" wailed Chris' mother. "Of course we understand! Do whatever you have to do! Call in any specialist you have to! We'll take care of whatever it costs...just do whatever you need to!"

"No, no. That won't be necessary." I said, trying to inject some calm into the situation. "I am going to put the baby on a very specialized fattening compound. It's a brand new formula that I discovered, and if...and I said if...everything goes well, he should be able to go home in four to six weeks."

"Oh thank-you! Thank you! Thank you doctor!"

And so it went. The announcements of Little Stamos' birth prominently mentioned his two pound one ounce birthweight, plus the fact that he had to be left in the hospital in an incubator constructed especially for very premature infants. Meanwhile, Chris and Adonis told everyone that the baby was receiving Dr. Kamen's special "fattening formula compound" that would quickly bring the baby's weight up.

Four weeks later, Little Stamos, duly "fattened," was ready to be displayed in the hospital nursery. Above the child's name plate in his isolette was a sign in large letters that read: "THIS BABY IS TO RECEIVE DR. KAMEN'S SPECIAL FATTENING COMPOUND ONLY." Anyone who could read saw it.

"My, my!" said Stamos' legion of admirers. "Dr. Kamen's compound must be extraordinary! Look at those fat little cheeks! Why, he looks positively plump!"

At the age of six weeks, Little Stamos was discharged. When he left the hospital, he weighed eight pounds, twelve ounces. Over the next two years, two more hefty premature babies born to other recently wed Greek parents were similarly isolated after birth and given my special "fattening" compound.

My Greek practice burgeoned.

EPILOGUE

Let there be no misunderstanding: A caper such as this one would most certainly not be tolerated in our present rigidly regulated medical environments. But this happened in the days when innovations designed to relieve non-medical problems and suffering was accepted by hospitals that dispensed compassion along with care.

Those were the days.

FAT SADIE

One thing should be clear before we begin: She wasn't always fat.

When she was born, Mary Beth Anne Murphy was of normal weight, a member of an Irish Catholic family so poor that they couldn't afford to feed and clothe her. By the age of three, she had gone from foster home to foster home, and orphanage to orphanage because of behavioral problems. She never remained in any one place for more than a few months. Abuse was hinted at, but not confirmed.

So it should come as no surprise that when she was but seventeen, she married Jesus, a strict Catholic Latino. She would really belong to someone...and perhaps have a place she could really call home. And her having a baby with Jesus was evidence of being bonded to another human. It would be a new life.

Her phenomenal weight gain began almost immediately following her civil marriage. Her food gorging would begin each morning and did not stop until she fell asleep at night. Incredibly, she consumed gargantuan amounts of food each day; Two to three dozen eggs, a pound of bacon for breakfast, whole loaves of bread, entire cakes, boxes of cookies and donuts, a dozen or more pork chops at a single sitting, a gallon of ice cream, bags of potato chips and on and on. When she turned nineteen, she had become the epitome of the medical term "morbidly obese."

The day I first met "Fat Sadie," I picked up her chart in the door pocket outside the examination room in my office. The nurse had put a large notation at the front of the chart: "NEW PATIENT— OBESE!!!" Right away, I knew that the patient who waited beyond the closed door did not have an ordinary weight problem, for "Auntie Jane," my office nurse, never made notations of that sort on a new patient's chart.

171

I must have gasped at the first sight of her...the most immense human being I had ever seen.

"I'm kinda fat, huh?"

I searched for the right words. I just stood there.

"Hello, Dr. Kamen. I'm Mary Beth Anne Ramirez, but you can call me 'Fat Sadie.' Everyone else does."

" Fat Sadie?" Even saying it made me uneasy.

"Oh sure, Doc. I don't mind, really. I know I'm fat, and Sadie is what Jesus calls me. Jesus, my husband. It's just a nickname, but it fits, huh?"

Fat Sadie had been standing in the corner of the examination room. As she walked across the room, I realized how enormous Fat Sadie was. She was headed for the chair, a well-built padded steel framed unit, but I had my doubts about it holding her when she sat down. We would soon find out. As she made her way across the room, I tried to estimate her total weight. 500...600...no...700 pounds...maybe more. She was the quintessential fat lady I had seen only in caricature or on a circus poster. I never imagined anyone that obese. I marveled, that she could walk. Amazingly, she didn't waddle. She walked with a normal gait. An awesome wonder.

She reached the chair, turned around and sat down. The chair held. Then she spoke.

"My husband will be here in just a minute," she began. "He wants to be here when we discuss my case."

Jesus appeared in the doorway. I turned to face him. The man was clinically skinny...rail thin...more bone than flesh. He and Fat Sadie were equal in height, both about 5'6" tall, but that was where their physical similarities ended. He was about as thick as

172

one of her thighs and leg. They were both ready for Barnum and Bailey.

"This is my husband Jesus, Dr. Kamen."

"Hello, Mr. Ramirez. Glad to meet you both."

Jesus nodded and gave me a weak handshake.

"You're wondering how he did it, huh?" asked Fat Sadie. "Well, if you are, that's OK, because everybody does. That's why he loves me this fat. He just loves to go on and brag and brag. He's a man's man you know and he loves it. Don't you?"

Jesus, whose hands were firmly planted in his pockets, shuffled, looked down and mumbled something inaudible. He managed a wan smile.

I turned to Fat Sadie.

"Mrs. Ramirez..." I began.

"Sadie, please," she corrected.

"Uh, Sadie," I continued. "What did you mean 'how he did it'?

There was a slight hesitation and a slight blush appeared.

"Why Doc, that's just why we're here! I thought your girl (my nurse) would have told you! I told her when she talked to me before I came in here. I'm pregnant."

"Uh, you're what?" I asked.

"Pregnant...you know...I'm going to have a baby."

I suppose that it's quite normal for physicians to feel fear during their careers when various crises arise. I often felt this when a horribly wounded or ill patient would come to Cook County Hospital when I was on Emergency Room call. I felt fear when I had to perform my first Caesarian Section all alone...or my first

173

cholecystectomy (gall bladder removal). But these fears were rational. This was bizarre.

"Uh, you WILL take me as a patient, won't you Dr. Kamen?"

I wanted to say no. Desperately, I searched for a way to tell her that she should find another doctor, that she should go to a medical center, that she needed someone more experienced.

She didn't give me a chance to say anything.

She continued. "Everyone...everyone I've gone to says no. Our family doctor won't even give me an appointment. We can't afford the specialist (OB/GYN) in Hammond, but I don't think he'd take me anyway. My neighbor told me about you. She's your patient. She said you were good in everything, that I wouldn't even need a specialist with you. Please, Dr. Kamen. Please take me!"

I just stared at her.

"Well, first off Sadie, how do you know you're pregnant?"

"Well Doc, how does any woman know she's pregnant? You just know! But mainly, I vomit all of the time, and I missed my period. Also, I feel heavy."

The last remark was incomprehensible.

"I just know I'm pregnant, Dr. Kamen."

I could not refuse to be her doctor. Trapped.

"Well, Sadie, I'll do the best I can, but I certainly can't promise anything. Above all, I can't promise that you'll make it or that the baby will make it. I'll just do the very best for you that I can."

Unhesitatingly: "We'll make it Doc!" she said smiling.

"Is this your first pregnancy?"

"The first. We've been trying for awhile though. You just gotta be patient and it happens, right Doc?"

"Uh, yeah. Yeah, sure." I wasn't really listening. I was trying to figure out what I had gotten into. First off, how was I going to do her pelvic examination? It had to be done...or at least attempted. With the help of Jesus and Margy, my other office nurse, we rolled another examination table into the room. When she entered the room, Margy saw Sadie for the first time. For an instant, she stopped pushing the table and gasped. Then she looked down and then, with a sense of apology, cleared her throat.

"Margy, this is Mrs. Ramirez. She's going to have a baby...I think."

Margy looked at Sadie, looked at me, and then at Jesus.

"Oh, and this is her husband, Jesus. We are going to do a pelvic exam on Mrs. Ramirez, Margy."

"Oh." Margy stood there.

"Now I've already told you. Call me Fat Sadie!"

Margy's eyes were widened. She looked dazed. Then: "I'll get a speculum."

Fat Sadie got up from the chair, and with surprising agility, climbed up on the examination tables that we fastened together with tape around the table legs. She laid on her back, covering both tabletops and spilling over the sides of each. The effort to examine was futile. As I had suspected. I could barely reach the womb. Her abdominal wall was much too thick to allow assessment of uterine size. I had to abandon hope of completing the procedure successfully, but I came away from the experience knowing with certainty what she had meant by "how he did it." I never asked her, nor do I know how he "did it."

Fat Sadie climbed off the tables.

"Well, Doc, how's it look? I'm right, ain't I?"

"Well, Sadie, I can't tell for sure. The opening to your womb...the cervix, is a bit soft so you might be pregnant but just to be sure, we'll do a rabbit test."

"OK, Doc. Suit yourself. But I am."

"And we'll have to weigh you and take your blood pressure."

"Uh Doc, there's no scale big enough. The supermarket scale where they weigh sides of beef only goes to 450 and I'm way more than that Doc. And no one can take my blood pressure."

Trouble. Big trouble.

"Well," I said. "The blood pressure shouldn't be too difficult. I'll get my widest cuff and use your forearm and feel for your pulse. Now for getting your weight...your weight...hm-m-m-m-m."

An idea. I went to the phone and looked up the telephone number of one of my patients who owned a lumber yard. I called him.

"Mr. Nichols?" I started. "This is Dr. Kamen. I'm calling from my office. Uh, what's the biggest scale you have down there at your place?"

"I got one here Doc that goes up all the way to six tons. Why?"

"No, that won't do." I said. "I need one that's more accurate to the pound. Do you have any smaller ones?"

"Well, I do have one that weighs to a thousand pounds. We use it for nail kegs."

"Great, that sounds like it would be perfect."

"What do you want it for?"

"Well, I have to weigh a patient. And I'll need to use it."

There was a long pause.

"Mr. Nichols, are you there?"

"Uh, yeah. You've got Fat Sadie, haven't you?"

"That's right."

"Thought so. Yeah sure, you can use it anytime, Doc."

"Thanks a lot. Oh, and Mr. Nichols, would you mind weighing her yourself and then calling me each time she comes in? I'm going to need her weight at least once a week."

"Happy to, Doc. Happy to. Anything else I can do for you, Doc?"

"Thanks again."

I sent her straight from the office to the lumber yard. Mr. Nichols called in with his first report later that afternoon. "602 pounds, Doc."

Later the next day, I heard from the lab.

The rabbit died. Sadie was going to have a baby.

•••••••••••••••••••••

Problems, not unexpected, began almost immediately. Though I had counseled her extensively on the dangers of gaining any more weight at all during her pregnancy, Mr. Nichols called me each week with news of another three, four, or five pound weight gain. I had even given Sadie sample daily menus as a guide, designed to provide her baby with sound nutrition while causing Sadie herself to lose weight. All to no avail.

She came into the office weekly to have her blood pressure taken by my nurse, Auntie Jane. That too showed a steady, incremental rise. Surprisingly, her first blood pressure reading was only modestly high at 150/90, but in two months it was life-threatening at 180/110. This was definite evidence of pre-eclampsia, a dangerous condition where the blood pressure rises, and the patient retains excessive amounts of water with potentially lethal consequences to the mother and baby. In full-blown toxemia of pregnancy, the mother can convulse and possibly die.

At that time, (the fifties), there were no strong diuretics and no medicines to safely lower blood pressure. The only treatments that could be expected to produce results were salt and calorie restriction. I had to think up a plan quickly, or else Sadie and the baby wouldn't survive. I called Sadie and asked her to bring Jesus in when she came to the office for her next weekly appointment. I was honest with her and told her that the situation was becoming more urgent each day. She said she understood, and would bring her husband in on Wednesday.

By this time, Fat Sadie was in her fifth month of pregnancy. As Sadie and Jesus sat across from me, I explained to them that Sadie had to go into the hospital immediately to be monitored, and put on a strict 1000 calorie a day diet. I had already discussed her case with the hospital dietitian who eagerly agreed to accept the challenge of saving Sadie's life and the life of her unborn child.

"This could be a real achievement, huh?" Miss Flannery, the dietitian asked. "I mean, she could lose a hundred pounds even before she has the baby, don't you think?" I appreciated her eagerness about the project, but I didn't want to be unrealistic. "Let's just do the very best we can."

I told Sadie and Jesus that Miss Flannery would be in charge of coming up with each day's menu, but that Sadie could make some choices with her. Miss Flannery would also work closely with her to rework her lifetime eating habits, so that she'd live a more normal dietetic life. I explained that this was our only chance to bring the pregnancy to a happy outcome. The proposition was readily accepted by Sadie and Jesus.

That afternoon, she was admitted to a medical floor. She soon became the pet of the unit. Nurses, lab techs, other patients, janitors...everyone found a reason to have to stop by her room and to root her on. When her meals were brought to her, she ate them uncomplainingly. She never asked for more, she ate slowly as directed by Mrs. Flannery, and she never badgered the staff or other patients for snacks...even for chocolate bars which she had confessed to me were her part of her downfall.

But Sadie continued to gain weight.

Every other day, the hospital truck would pick her up and transport her to the lumber yard, and every day, the news logged was bad. In one week, she'd gained eight pounds. It was time for yet stricter measures.

All visitors, except for Jesus, were banned from Sadie's room. There was a sign posted on her bed to that effect, explaining that Mrs. Ramirez was on a "VERY RESTRICTED DIET."

But even this was for naught. The following week, she gained six more pounds.

All caregivers were confounded. It was inconceivable that she should be gaining any weight on the diet she was on. But all were at a loss to solve the mystery. It was one of the nun nurses at the hospital who finally solved the problem.

The nun had noticed that when Jesus would visit each evening after work, he would be carrying a large locker bag with him. When she asked him about the bag during his first visit, he told her that it contained his work clothes.

"I like to change into something clean after work." he said.

For awhile, no more was ever said about it. During one of his visits, however, the Sister noticed something peculiar about the bag. The one he brought with him at night was dark blue. But the one he left with, although the same size, was powder blue. What was going on here? Then the Sister sprang into action. It was time to play sleuth.

The following evening, before Jesus could go into her room, the Sister seized the bag from him...despite his protestations to the contrary. His swearing could not deter her from finding out what was in the bag. Inside, the cache was revealed. It included two dozen pork chops, barbecued and still warm, a large bottle of Coca-Cola, and a few unopened bags of Oreo cookies.

The Sister telephoned me with the news.

Within one hour, I transferred Fat Sadie out of the medical floor and put her in "the cage," a hospital room used to house prisoners who were ill, but in police custody. All windows and doors were covered with heavy metal wire mesh. The door was solid and had a large padlock. It was a desperate move for desperate times. I instructed the nursing staff that only the charge nurse herself and no one else was to have access to the key. She alone would be responsible for allowing admittance to hospital personnel. All visitors, especially Jesus, had to remain on the outside and talk to Sadie through the wire mesh.

Mrs. Flannery, the dietitian, was happy to learn why her star patient had gained all that weight under her careful supervision. She had been depressed over the situation and her seeming ineffectiveness at getting Sadie's weight down. Upon hearing of the newest arrangement however, she was newly energized and was excited to give it yet another "go."

It worked. In six weeks time, Sadie lost ninety pounds.

•••••••••••••••••••••

I should have known better.

Christmas was coming and Sadie begged me to let her go home for the holidays.

"Please Dr. Kamen, oh please!" came her repeated pleas. "Just for a couple of days. Remember, you said I might die so I want to spend my last Christmas at home with my family. Please Dr. Kamen! Please!"

Reluctantly, I relented and gave her a two-day pass. Two days. Thursday and Friday. How much damage could she possibly do in two days? She promised that she would be good and remain on her diet.

When she returned, she had regained eighteen pounds!! She went back into "the cage" immediately. Instead of 1000 calories a day, she was placed on a 900 calorie a day diet. I, and the nursing staff, were determined.

Pitiful wailing. The nurses, disturbed by her constant moaning, repeatedly asked me to give her back at least the 100 calories a day that she had lost. But I held firm. There was no going back now. They would either have to put up with it or wear earplugs. Nine-hundred calories a day. No more than that.

The weight loss was phenomenal. As Sadie approached her due date, she was weighing in at a comparatively svelte 460 pounds. (Another 10 pounds and we could begin going to the supermarket to weigh her.) The time had now come to start worrying about the actual delivery.

I met with Sister Carletta, the OB supervisor, to plan the delivery. Together, we tried to anticipate every possible complication that could arise during her labor and delivery. We went so far as to set up a complete surgical facility in the delivery room if a Caesarian Section became necessary. We even contemplated an elective (planned) C-section, but the obstetric consultant felt that the risk of such a procedure would be too great and recommended a trial vaginal delivery.

Her pelvis could be a problem. It was the bony pelvis opening which could be inadequate for the size of the baby's head. I ordered an x-ray pelvimetry, which would allow the radiologist to determine if there was a head to pelvis disproportion. If so, then a C-section would be mandatory.

A call from the radiologist came during my afternoon office hours. Dr. Sam Levin and I had been good friends since I arrived at St. Catherine's hospital, so there were no formalities on his part.

"Well, Yankel (my Yiddish name)," he began. "You're in a real pile of dreck (feces) now."

"And why, may I ask, do you say so?" I said jokingly.

"Because, my good friend, I hear you've had this patient in the hospital for about four months now with a diagnosis of pre-toxemia. You've spent umpteen thousands of dollars of the insurance company's money, you've been driving the nurses and security nuts with this woman, and..."

"Nu, nu...Shimshon (his Yiddish name), get to the point."

"And Yankele," he resumed. "She's not even pregnant."

"Look, Sam, Shimshon...Dr. Levin—don't give me a hard time. Just because your technicians don't know how to take an x-ray, that doesn't make her unpregnant."

"Look, Dr. Kamen—I did something I haven't done in twenty years. I went up and examined your patient. I can't feel her uterus."

"Listen, you couldn't feel if she had two basketballs in there. Let me explain something to you. As you probably noticed, the woman is big. B-I-G, big! H-U-G-E. M-A-S-S-I-V-E."

"Alright, alright. Enough with the spelling lesson. I'll try again."

"Good, Sam. Call me."

By the time his next call came, his tone was decidedly different. He sounded less triumphant more to the point.

"Yankele." We were friends again. "I really had to give her the juice to get the picture, but, uh, there is no cephalo-pelvic disproportion. The head will fit through."

"Gottsu danken. (Thank God). Shimshon, thanks a lot. You've been a tremendous help."

"My pleasure, as always, Yankele." He hung up chuckling.

•••••••••••••••••••••••

The call from OB came at the worst possible time. It was two o'clock in the morning. That's the time of night when the fewest hospital personnel are available, and it takes the mind a good deal longer to think rationally.

"Hello, Dr. Kamen. This is Mrs. Greene up on OB. Mrs. Ramirez' water bag has broken and she's having five-minute pains...started about two hours ago. I'm sending her to OB delivery right now." She sounded nervous.

"Thank you. I'm leaving right now."

I arrived at the hospital about twenty minutes later. The plan that Sister Carletta and I had outlined was already in effect.

Sadie was taken directly into the delivery room on only one cart, but with an orderly on either side holding her. She was then transferred to two delivery tables that had been bolted together by the maintenance department. It was impossible to use stirrups. Large non-skid gym shoes were put on her feet so she could press against the tabletops in order to push.

Four nurse's aides were called in to assist. I was praying.

The staff was now working as a team. The first thing we had to do was attach large adhesive straps to the upper inner part of her thighs and to the skin of the lower abdomen. Each aide was then assigned to hold a strap, and on my cue, they were told to pull. That would force the fat out of the way so the baby could emerge.

Though the head had not yet crowned (appeared in the vaginal opening), we rehearsed the maneuver. When I said "PULL!" all pulled in unison! The fat of the thighs was drawn away and the huge fatty abdominal "apron" was drawn upwards. For the first time since she came into my care, I had access to the vagina.

So there we all were in the delivery room: myself, Sister Carletta, the nurses, the aides, and two orderlies...all cheering her on through each contraction and all waiting anxiously for the birth.

"Come on Sadie!!! Come on sweetheart! You can do it! Just a few more pushes and then you'll have your baby!" The team coaxed her.

Sadie pushed mightily. With each contraction, she bore down with such force that her face burned bright red. Sweat poured from everywhere and with each contraction, she had great gutteral groans. Anyone unoccupied in the delivery room not holding one of the straps, helped to hold Sadie's shoulders up as she pushed and grunted her way through two hours of strong, sustained contractions. With each contraction, little, but some, progress was made. Her neck and hemmorhoidal veins were bulging from all the pushing.

Then...the head suddenly began to appear.

"Push Sadie, push!!" I shouted. "A little more...a little more...that's it Sadie! That's it!"

"I can't no more Doc! I can't!" she cried.

"Now don't quit now Sadie! Here comes another contraction...now close your mouth and push as hard as you can and this should be your last push...come on Sadie...now PUSH!!!!!"

Sadie managed a faint smile, then did as I told her. With unbelievable force, she bore down for what seemed like at least an entire minute.

Then with one final grunt, the head was born.

Cries of triumph went up throughout the delivery room. Whooping and yelling, "You did it! You did it!" echoed throughout.

Then...near catastrophe.

Just as my friend Sam, the radiologist, had predicted, there was indeed sufficient room for the head to pass through the bony canal, but now the shoulders of the baby stuck.

The baby's size was apparently very large. The non-bony tissues of Sadie's birth canal could not allow enough room for the shoulders of the child to pass through. There was just too much fat and no way at all to displace it.

I attempted every maneuver I'd ever been taught. Nothing. The baby didn't budge. I certainly did not want to harm the nerves of the arms that come from the neck area, but I pulled and tugged as much as I could without harming it. Not an inch of progress could be made. Time was running out quickly.

I suddenly remembered, in a postgraduate lecture in Denver I had attended about two years before, hearing the speaker discuss such a predicament. "If all else fails," I could hear him say. "Break the clavicle."

Break the clavicle...the bone that goes from the upper breast bone to the shoulder. I had never done it. Geez, how do you do it? How do you break the baby's clavicle? There wasn't enough time to even make a phone call to find out. The baby was becoming dusky, evidence that it needed oxygen. The baby needed to breathe immediately.

I took my thumb and pushed in the center of the left clavicle. Initially, I felt it bend, and then...crack.

I still couldn't extract the baby.

I placed my thumb in the center of the right clavicle. It cracked easily.

Immediately, both shoulders collapsed inward and the body slipped out easily. I put a gauze over its mouth and blew a few times. It gasped once...a small quick gasp...and then again...and again... and then it cried...at first weakly...then lustily.

There was cheering in the delivery room.

"Sadie! You've got yourself a little boy!" I was proud and exhausted.

Sadie smiled, then started to sob. It was a few minutes before she regained her composure.

"Oh Dr. Kamen," she cried, "This is the only good I've ever done in my life. The only time I can ever remember being happy...I'm not a freak, am I Doc? I did good, didn't I? I did like normal, didn't I?" The sobbing returned.

"Mary Beth Anne Ramirez...you are definitely not a freak, and not only did you do good, you did great! We're all with you, but best of all, you're with us...and your beautiful baby boy is with us. You have everything to be happy about."

It took about ten minutes to repair some minor tears that occurred during the delivery. But before I could leave the delivery room, she called me over once more.

"Doc, you know, I've been thinking."

"Yes?"

"This whole thing...I mean having a baby and all...it wasn't really so bad after all. How soon can we try for another one?"

"We'll have to talk about this later, Mary Beth Anne. Much later."

"OK, Doc. But you can betcha...we are going to talk."

I smiled and Sadie smiled back. I patted her shoulder and left.

•••••••••••••••

The baby, named Jesus John, Jr., did very well. The broken clavicles healed without incident, and Sadie and the baby were discharged in a few days. But a few weeks later, when Sadie brought "J.J." in for a six-week check-up, she was crying and distraught. My first thought was that she was having a bout of post-partum depression. But I was wrong. She told me Jesus had walked out on her and the baby.

Jesus, having demonstrated his virility and apparent sexual prowess, concluded that assuming the responsibility of raising and providing for his son just wasn't to be. He left one day without explanation the week after she was discharged from the hospital. He just announced that he was leaving and wouldn't be back, having made no provision for the support of his family. He packed a few things, took his radio, and the small TV set. Then he was gone.

It was a dispirited Sadie who sat in my office that day, cradling the baby and sobbing. In broken sentences punctuated with fits of wailing, she recounted her latest misfortune, and ended by saying she didn't know how she was going to pay me.

"I'm not going on charity or welfare, Dr. Kamen. I just can't do it." she cried. "I am going to get a job, and then I'll pay you. I promise."

"Don't worry about paying me." I told her. "But what kind of a job can you possibly get right now Mary Beth Anne? I think you need to face some things here, and go on welfare...just for the time being, of course. You need money for food, for rent...and of course for the baby. Mary Beth Anne, who's going to hire you? Do you have any prospects for a decent job?"

Suddenly, she smiled and brightened.

"Oh, Dr. Kamen, I already HAVE a job. I'm just waiting 'til they fix it up."

"You have a job? What kind of job? And what are they fixing up?"

"I'm going to drive a taxi-cab."

I was bewildered. She continued.

"I know what you're thinking, Dr. Kamen. I don't mind. You're thinking about how I can't possibly drive a cab when you don't think I can fit into it. You're thinking the cab won't hold. And you don't know why anyone would give me a job like that.

"But let me tell you, that's exactly what they're fixing up." she continued. "Mr. Stash Yankovic (the owner of the local cab company in town) has this old Buick station wagon and he's putting on the wider door from a 2-door Buick Regal and he's putting in a real wide seat. He said he'll put on truck springs and suspensions, and move the passenger seat back and..."

The torrent of words continued until she had explained all she knew of the taxi-cab modifications that were being completed for her.

188

"Wait a minute, Mary Beth Anne," I said. "Why would Stash go to all this trouble and expense? Not that I don't think it's great, but he's a guy who wants, like everybody else, to turn a buck."

"Well I'll tell you why." she said, sitting up straight in her chair. "I once worked as a dispatcher for him for about a year and a half, and Stash and I...we got along great. When I called him and asked him if I could have my job back, he said it was filled, and then he was the one who thought of this. He said that everybody would want to ride in my cab. Everybody! So I said I would do it."

"And who's going to take care of J.J.?"

At once, she turned mournful. A melancholy mask drew over her face. Her rotund features that moments before had been sparkling now sagged as tears silently formed and fell down her cheeks.

"I'm going to give him up for adoption."

This was so wholly unexpected. It was lamentable, tragic, deplorable.

"Oh Mary Beth Anne, you can't! You can't!" I could think of nothing else to say.

"Oh Dr. Kamen, I've got to! What other choice do I have? Look at me! Look at me! Do you think anyone would ever want me as a mother? It's what's best for J.J. Look! Look at me!!!" She broke down in unrestrained fits of crying.

I went over to her and patted her on the shoulder.

"You're wrong, Mary Beth Anne. I...I...I think you're going to make a wonderful mother for J.J. I mean it...I truly mean it. Please, don't do anything just yet. Give me a chance to work on it. Will you do that? Will you give me a week?"

Sadie looked at me and sighed.

"OK, Dr. Kamen. OK," she said, the tears finally subsiding.

As soon as Sadie left the office, I called Dorothy Neufeld, the executive secretary of Catholic Charities, the umbrella organization of all the local Catholic services. She owed me a favor, and I was going to collect. I was the physician for the local orphan home of the Catholic Adoption Services, and I was the physician for the nuns of the Catechism School. I did this without charge. Now, I wanted payment in-kind.

I told Miss Neufeld about Mary Ann's plight. She listened attentively, acknowledging what I was telling her with an "I see, uh-huh, I see."

"And she's Catholic, I presume." Miss Neufeld said after I had finished.

"If she isn't, she will be in about a half an hour," I said. Miss Neufeld laughed. (Surprising, since she was always about business.)

"I don't think this is going to be a problem," she said. "I'll work something out."

And work something out she did. Her solution proved to be a *tour de force* for Catholic Charities, for it was Sadie's situation that propelled them into inaugurating the concept of organized day care. At the time, such an entity was virtually unheard of. Miss Neufeld called it "Daytime Foster Care " and it worked. Under the program, Sadie would be able to drop off J.J. in the morning, and then pick him up after her shift. Sadie was thrilled, and agreed to abandon any idea of putting J.J. up for adoption.

So Sadie went to work for Stash driving her specially reinforced cab. Soon, she was able to provide a significant portion of J.J.'s day care expenses herself because she became the busiest driver ever in the history of The Yankovich Cab Company. She was making more money than any other driver in the company, even though Stash kept 60% of her receipts to offset the cost of her cab modifications.

Sadie's tips were great. Everyone wanted to ride with Sadie, and it was a status thing to be seen in her cab. It even became a custom for Sadie to transport a bride and her family to the church. People said it was good luck...very good luck. And often, "send Fat Sadie...only Fat Sadie" was what the dispatcher heard when parents ,who were taking their newborns home from the hospital, called Yankovich's for a cab. Even business executives at the local steel mills would ask for Sadie to pick up their out-of-town clients or visiting administrators. It was always a springboard for conversation. It was understood that her tips for these "specials" would be princely. After all, it was luck...good luck...very good luck to ride with Sadie and to tip her generously.

And so it went for about three years. She prospered, moved into a nice apartment, and cared for little (but getting bigger all the time) J.J. But suddenly, her prodigious luck failed her. Sadie's cab broke down, and like the one horseshoe, it was irreparable....gone...kaput.

In the meantime, Stash's business had grown, in no small part due to Sadie's popularity. He became a franchisee of the Yellow Cab Company, which frowned on "antics" or "stunts." The parent firm insisted that business always be conducted with dignity and decorum. A "proper image" must be maintained. Though local business leaders, clergy, and others in the community intervened on Sadie's behalf, it was all to no avail. Sadie's days as a cabbie were over.

Her phone call to me had a sense of finality and desperation. She called to enlist my help in finding her a job right away.

"I'll do anything, Dr. Kamen! Anything! Do you know anyone I can talk to? Please help me! What am I going to do?"

Any help I could give Sadie was limited, at best. I and my office personnel made phone calls. We took up money collections, which she would not accept. We collected food for her and her child which she did take. But as for a job, no luck.

Three months later, however, Sadie came in with J.J. for his final innoculation booster. She was very well-dressed in an outfit that was conspicuously expensive and custom-made, of course, for there were no "off the rack" clothes made in her size. She wore a perky pill-box felt hat with a small dart of an ecru-colored feather pointing upward. Her shoes were of the finest patent leather and each had a large silver buckle. She smiled when she saw me.

"You look great, Mary Beth Anne!" I said. "Let me guess. You got another job."

"I sure did, Dr. Kamen, and this one is the best yet! In fact, now I can take care of J.J. all by myself. Well...not completely by myself, but I only have help once in a while."

"Well tell me, Mary Beth Anne, what kind of work are you doing?"

She hesitated for a moment. Then she spoke.

"Well-l-l-l-l...it's kind of providing domestic services. But I do business out of my apartment."

Domestic services. I figured she was taking in washing, ironing, and sewing. It seemed reasonable enough, but she did appear to be making a large amount of money for performing small "domestic services." I was, however, unfamiliar with the going rates. Maybe this was apparently more lucrative than driving the cab. But it was a bizarre event that took place two days later that revealed the true nature of her "domestic services."

I was in the office finishing with my last patient of the day when I got the call.

"Hello, Doc. This is Irwin. Thank Goodness you're in. I've got a problem I'll bet you've never seen. Thank God you're still there. I'll be right up."

Irwin Goldman had his pharmacy a block north of my office. I met him on my first day of practice, and Shirley and I had become quite close with him and Christina, his English Evangelical wife who never did convert to his Judaism. He had three children who were being raised as Jews. A fine, solid, staid family man.

Five minutes later, Irwin opened the door to my office and stood there. For a moment, I didn't know who it was because he had a newspaper hiding his face. It was only when he lowered the paper that I was able to recognize him.

The first thing I noticed was that he had two 2-inch black, wriggly worm-like animals hanging from each lower eyelid. His hair was totally disheveled and his nose was bleeding. Periodically, he dabbed some blood that was oozing from the corner of his mouth.

"Irwin! What the hell happened to you? Wait...I know what happened, but why, Irwin, why? And what are those things hanging on your cheeks?"

"They're leeches, Jack. Medicinal leeches. I still sell them to some of my *old country* patients. I put them on to get rid of these damn black eyes, but I can't get them off. They really suck the blood out of you, don't they?"

"Irwin, what do you expect me to do? I've never worked with leeches before, and I've never seen any that size! I got a couple of small ones on me at summer camp once, but I just pulled them off."

"Look, Jack, operate...do anything! But for God's sake, get them off of me!!"

Then I remembered—light a match under a leech and it'll let go. A myth? I tried it and it worked. The blood engorged leeches curled up and came off quite easily. Then Irwin sat down.

"Aw, thanks Jack. I didn't know what I was going to do."

"Alright, Irwin. Now tell me. Who made you into hamburger?"

"Well, you know Jesus Ramirez, that little..."

"Sure I know him," I said. "He's the ex-husband of one of my patients. Don't tell me that little guy did this to you!"

"Yeah...him and two of his buddies. I thought they were going to kill me for sure."

"Uh, Irwin, can I ask why?"

"Why? I had his ex, that's why."

I was speechless.

"What's wrong, Jack? What, you think everybody's like you? You're the one that's not normal, you know that?"

I finally found my voice again.

"Why did Jesus do this? He's not married to Sadie anymore. Why should he care who she sleeps with?"

"Jack, it's because I paid her and not him. I gave HER the fifty bucks. I didn't know that she didn't give him his cut."

Her pimp. Jesus was her pimp.

"Uh, Jack, don't tell me you didn't know."

"No, Irwin, I didn't know. I didn't know any of this. None of it."

"Well, like it or not, that's how it is, Jack. And then, after he and his buddy worked my up good, he says it's going to cost me 100 bucks from now on. Can you imagine that? He thinks I want to
194

screw her again! Hell, I just wanted it once, like everyone else...you know, just to see if I could do it."

Irwin sat there in my office and shrugged his shoulders. "That's just the way it is, Jack. That's just the way it is."

He used the mirror in my bathroom to comb his hair and wash his face. He had grabbed some makeup foundation from his store that he dabbed under his eyes. Satisfied that he looked the best he was going to look in his situation, he turned to leave.

"Yep, Jack, that's just the way it is."

Shirley and I never saw much of Irwin and Christina after that. And Sadie didn't call or come into the office until about a year later. J.J. had fallen and cut his elbow. The gash wasn't deep or large enough to make a trip to the Emergency Room, but it needed some medical attention.

Sadie came into the examination room cheerful and eager to greet me again after so long a time, but I was silent, attending only to J.J.'s wound. I still harbored this hurt. It was like a feeling of betrayal.

Alone with Sadie and J.J., she finally addressed my coolness.

"What's wrong, Doc. Ain'tcha talkin'?"

I looked at her. She was as enormous as ever. Over the year, I had forgotten exactly how huge she was, but now, seeing her holding J.J. against her breast, her weight again imprinted itself.

"To tell the truth, Mary Beth Anne, I'm horribly disappointed. I thought you had more going for you. I really did."

"Whaddaya mean, Doc? Whaddaya mean?"

"I mean, Mary Beth Anne, that you're a prostitute, or to put it another way...you're a whore. That's what I mean."

My remarks didn't seem to faze her. She straightened, drawing herself up to full rotundity, and tilted her head backwards.

"I beg your pardon, Doctor Jack Kamen. I didn't realize you were a saint. A real saint."

She was angry. Her teeth clenched.

"And besides," she continued. "I am NOT a whore. So what do you think of THAT?"

"Look, Mary Beth Anne. It's all over town. What about these buttons I'm seeing around town on young punks that say, 'I've seen Sadie'? What does THAT mean?"

"What that means," she began, almost shaking with rage, "is that all of that is in my past. I just told you I'm not a whore...at least not anymore. Not for three or four months now. I own my own place now, thank you. I have my own girls."

"You WHAT?!!!"

"I have my own girls that work only for me. Not one walker. All in my house."

"What about Jesus?"

"What about him? Aw, the poor guy. He had a little accident. I figured out that I didn't need him. He said I did and I said I didn't. Then he had the accident."

"A car accident?"

"Unh-unh. I think he was mugged. He got beaten up real bad. Anyway, he's gone...went back to Puerto Rico. I think he thinks it's just too dangerous here." She chortled.

I said no more then or ever again about her occupation. But before she left, she gave me a brown envelope. I opened it over my desk, and out came a large gold-plated key.

"Doc," she explained. "I'm going to use you for all my girls, but I don't want you to stop in the bar to get the key to call me at night for the key. So this is for you. You know you have the honor of being the only doctor to ever have the key to the whorehouse. Oh, and Doc...use it any way you want to."

EPILOGUE

I made several medical calls on her "girls" before I left family practice several years later.

Ordinarily, the male customer would stop in the cocktail lounge that occupied the ground level and purchase a key. A small bell would ring when he opened the door and the girls would "present" themselves on the second floor landing. Then the "chosen" one would keep the key that she would eventually redeem to Sadie for her fee.

However, it was cries of, "It's only Doc!" that greeted me when I used my key.

Demoralizing.

About twelve years later, I heard that Sadie died of complications due to her extreme obesity. Periodically, I would run into her son, J.J. Today, he is a massive, but muscular man, but not nearly as obese as his mother was. He is a gentle man, with a soft voice that seems incongruous with his girth. But whenever I see him, he never fails to speak lovingly of the memory of his mother, Mary Beth Anne Ramirez.

"She never minded when people called her Fat Sadie, Dr. Kamen," he once told me. "But she said you'd never call her that. She said you called her just Sadie or Mary Beth Anne. And she said you respected her too, Dr. Kamen. The way she saw it, not many other people did."

No, Mary Beth Anne, you're not a freak. It's the rest of us that may need some help.

Rest in peace.

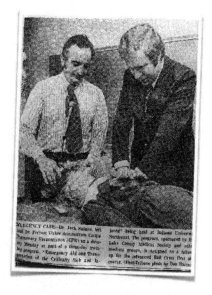

(L): Dad was appointed to the Gary Board of Health in 1972.

ABOVE: Dad demonstrating CPR at Indiana University Northwest in 1972.

DR. MILFORD

The Intensive Care Unit had only been open for one month when I got the call in the early morning hours. Mrs. Floyd, the night nursing supervisor was on the phone.

"Oh, Dr. Kamen," she began, her voice cracking with nervous laughter. "I, uh...I, uh..." More laughter and tittering. It was awhile before she could speak again...or even try. I heard sporadic bursts of giggling. Silence.

The she started again. "Oh, Dr. Kamen, it was just awful! I mean, uh...it IS awful! I mean...we really don't know what to do...uh, what I mean is, you'd better come down here now!" Another burst of uncontrolled laughter.

"Mrs. Floyd, please tell me what happened! Which bed is it? What is so hilariously funny about something that's so awful!"

She was trying to compose an answer, but always erupted into laughter that thwarted any effort by her to stifle it.

"Look, Florence," I said. "At least control yourself long enough to tell me who the patient is!"

I heard coughing. The words come out in short gasps.

"Oh, Dr. Kamen! I...I...I...don't know...I can't..." Her laughter had completely taken over. Finally, she gave the phone to the floor nurse.

"Hello, Dr. Kamen. This is Mrs. Danzig."

"Yes, Tina."

"Dr. Kamen, what happened IS awful, like Mrs. Floyd said, but it isn't a patient."

"Not a patient?"

"No. It's...it's..." Uproarious laughter. It appeared that Mrs. Floyd was contagious.

Mrs. Danzig resumed talking.

"Dr. Kamen, it's not a patient. It's...it's...Dr. Milford!!!!"

Burst of laughter.

"Look, Tina, can you people please tell me what happened? Tell me what's so funny—what's so awful. It's 1:30 am!"

"Trust me, Dr. Kamen." said Mrs. Danzig. "No one will be able to tell you over the phone what's happened, but you'd better come down. But we warned him, Dr. Kamen. We warned him. WE did just what you taught us, and we warned him about what you said, but he didn't listen. Just like always, he didn't listen. Oh, and by the way, bed eight died."

That was Mr. Mathers. At eighty-two, he had suffered a massive stroke and his death overnight was expected. But it wasn't Mr. Mathers that I was going to see at 1:30 in the morning. Heck, I didn't yet know who or what I was giving up sleep for, but it sounded intriguing enough to get me up. On my way to the hospital, I imagined several scenarios as to what might have occurred. I attributed the lateness of the hour and my lack of proper rest for my inability to solve the puzzle.

Dr. Milford. Dr. Mason Milford was on duty in the Emergency Room. It was his night for taking call. He had probably been called to ICU by the charge nurse because bed eight was bad. OK, so then what? What could have happened to him that was so awful, and yet apparently so funny? What had happened?

It was around 2 a.m. when I arrived at the ICU. At that hour of the morning, the only entrance into the hospital was through the Emergency Room. Security personnel were ever-present, and regardless of the time of day or night, the place was always bustling.

I parked my car in one of the "Physicians Only" spaces. The place was jammed. Patients and their anxious friends and relatives were everywhere...on the chairs, on the floor, and with the overflow in the hallway, just outside the waiting room. An ER nurse was trying to assure a nervous mother that she was trying as hard as she could to get a doctor to see her baby. Another nurse was putting a gauze dressing on a bleeding finger belonging to the apparent loser of a domestic argument. I looked around, trying to determine why so many patients had been allowed to congregate in the ER, and why no one was being seen by an M.D. I approached one of the nurses.

"Where's Milford? Why aren't any of these patients being seen?"

The nurse applying the finger dressing quickly finished her work and then motioned for me to step a few feet away from the patients. She began:

"Uh, Dr. Milford is being treated right now in ER Exam 1."

I turned towards the room and started to go. The nurse caught my arm.

"Dr. Kamen, Dr, Milford doesn't want anyone else in there. Dr. Salva is in with him now."

"Salva? The urologist?"

"Yes. But I mean it, Dr. Kamen. I wouldn't go in there if I were you. He means it. He even called in his partner, Dr. Silder, and he's on his way. He's taking over his ER call for the rest of the night."

I headed straight for the ICU. As I came through the double doors, I noticed that all of the nurses were gathered at the chart desk...with one of them carefully watching the patients' monitors. All the others were laughing and giggling.

"Oh, good!" said Mrs. Floyd. "Are we ever glad you're here. But now that we think about it, you really didn't have to come, but just the same, I think it's best because this way, we get to tell you OUR side of the story. I'm sure he'll tell you something else, but listen. Doctor, we're going to tell you what REALLY happened."

I really didn't have to come in? So what was I doing there? I hadn't gotten to bed until after 11 p.m., I was called at 1:30, and then I was told I didn't really need to come after all.

"Florence, let's go into the backroom and get some coffee and talk about this. Then for God's sake, tell me exactly what is going on!"

Mrs. Floyd and I went back into the small nurse's lounge next to the chart desk area. I poured coffee for both of us.

Well, Dr. Kamen," she began, "You know Dr. Milford? You know the way he is? You know how hardheaded he can be?"

Yes, I knew him and she was right. He was an obstinate man. He was under the assumption that he knew everything about everything, and more than he ever needed to know about all things medical. He was the only one of the ER physicians who refused to attend the cardio-pulmonary resuscitation course that I and my ICU co-director taught. He said that he'd "already read about it and I damn well know exactly what to do and don't need to take your damn course."

More than once, he ordered cardiac drugs inappropriately, largely because he was unable to properly read an EKG. (He never bothered to take that course either.) He also refused to learn how to intubate, (insert a breathing device) into a patient's airway. He said any fool could do it.

He was a physician disliked by both the nursing staff and his physician colleagues who mostly resented his haughtiness. Regardless, the man had a thriving practice in general family medicine, and it was probably because his self-adulation was mistaken for supreme confidence and authoritativeness.

"Well, it all started when bed eight died." Mrs. Floyd continued.

"It started WHEN he died? Not before?" I asked.

"Yes. It started when he died. You know Mr. Mathers...he had the massive stroke."

"Yes, I know."

"OK, so we called the ER to have the doctor on call come down to the unit to pronounce him so that we could call the funeral home."

"Yes."

"Well, Dr. Milford was on call."

"Go on."

"Yes, well he came down here, but it took him about fifteen minutes."

"And then?"

"Well then that's when it all started.He walked over to the patient and looked at the EKG and said that Mathers' heart was still active!"

"And was it?"

"Of course not! Look, I've got the strip here. There's just a little artifact on it, but certainly no cardiac activity."

I took the strip and studied it. Mrs. Floyd was right, of course. There was no cardiac activity. An EKG will sometimes show spurious changes caused by electrical interferences present in the area. But these "artifacts" are distinctly different in character from true cardiac-generated input.

"OK, Mrs. Floyd. Then?"

"So what happened? All hell broke loose is what happened. He started ranting and screaming that we could still save him...that we didn't know what we were doing...that we were incompetent...that we were..."

"Alright, alright, I get the picture. What happened then?"

"Well then he ordered all kinds of crazy stuff. He ordered two more IV's, he ordered IV drugs. He was grabbing wildly for everything in sight. So he grabbed for an IV bag and was trying to hang it up and it broke, so the whole front of him got soaked in saline solution."

"Yes."

"And then that's when that awful thing I told you about happened."

"What awful thing? You didn't tell me what happened...remember?"

"Oh yeah, that's right. Well, he said he was going to shock the patient to restart the heart and to give him a normal rhythm."

"Strange."

"Not as weird as what happened. You see, he took the paddles and told us to charge up the defibrillator, which we did."

"And then?"

"And then, he bent over the metal railing which was still up and his body was touching the metal railing...and remember he was soaked and the patient also got soaked. All the nurses were yelling to each other to stand back...just stand back just like you taught us

Dr. Kamen. Do you remember? You said that before you shock anyone, no one should touch the patient or the bed and stand back."

"Yes."

"Well I don't think he took your course, and he sure didn't pay any attention to what any of us were saying. In fact, Sally told him specifically to stand back. He just gave her this real nasty look and said, 'Look, I know what I'm doing. Butt out!!'"

"Oh no...I can see it coming. What happened?"

"Well, then as I said, all hell broke loose...I mean REALLY broke loose! He pushed the buttons and all of the sudden he gave out the most God-awful yell I ever heard. It must have scared the other patients in the unit. I know it sure scared the hell out of me. I was standing right next to him. I tell you Dr. Kamen, he must have jumped 4, 5 or even 6 feet straight up, because we all realized that the shock had gone right to his...uh...his..."

"Genitals?"

"That's it. He shocked the hell out of his genitals."

That was all I needed to hear. Suddenly, coming down to hospital at 1:30 in the morning was worth it just to hear the story. Yes, I know, in retrospect, it really isn't funny, but at that instant, it was funny. Trust me. Hilarious. It became impossible for me to control myself. Mrs. Floyd and I were in the lounge, both laughing uncontrollably. The other nurses came into the lounge to join us. Anyone walking in on the scene would have thought we had gone mad. Finally, I managed to speak again."

"So what happened next?"

"Well, he started to do the weirdest dance I've ever seen. He immediately grabbed his genitals and he was screaming and dancing and jumping and yelling. Then he accused us of stepping

205

up the juice on the defibrillator on purpose, and then he ran out of here still holding on to his, uh..."

"Genitals."

"Right, his genitals."

EPILOGUE

Despite Dr. Milford's valiant efforts, Mr. Mathers was still, unfortunately, dead. I pronounced him and the funeral home was called.

Dr. Milford remained in the ER with Dr. Salva for a long time...at least two or three hours. I am certain that no permanent damage resulted to Dr. Milford's genitals, though I can't verify it.

The story of what had happened in the ICU that night quickly spread throughout the hospital. Dr. Milford took a few days off and then returned to work, tight-lipped. Clearly, he wasn't about to discuss the matter. But despite his near-fatal incident, Dr. Milford still refused to take the CPR course, and he refused to ever again enter or treat anyone in the ICU.

Good. But that incident was spoken of for several years. Jerry Lee Lewis even had a hit record once called, "Great Balls o' Fire"." But it was just coincidence.

THE LADIES AUXILIARY

"You're trying very hard not to work here, aren't you, Dr. Kamen?"

Sister Anna Theresa, the Mother Superior, was in a bad mood. A very bad mood. I knew she meant business.

Trouble. Deep trouble.

"I've always—since the first day that you joined this staff— I've always tried to protect you Dr. Kamen. Why? Sometimes I don't know myself, but I've always considered you to be a good doctor. Compassionate and, but if you'll excuse my saying so...crazy. Your escapades may occasionally be humorous to you and perhaps to some of our nursing staff, but I assure you, they are not funny to me. Still, I've protected you. I've canceled disciplinary meetings when your name appeared on the agenda. I've done everything I could, but now, Dr. Kamen, I think I've reached my limit."

"Uh, Sister, you know maybe it would help if you'd give me a hint as to what others might have imagined I've done. As far as I know, I haven't done anything that you would consider offbeat for at least two or three weeks."

"Oh, you haven't, have you?" she said, removing her glasses and moving them forward towards me across the desk. "You *think* you haven't. Let me put it this way. There are seven members on the governing board of this hospital and four out of the seven are gunning for you. They want you out as Director of Intensive Care. They want you out as Director of Pulmonary Services. They want you out as a member of the Executive Committee. And if they could, the'd vote you right out of the hospital."

"Oh. Could it be that they're upset at something I've done?"

"*Are they upset??!!!*" She couldn't finish. Usually, Sister Anna Theresa's voice was controlled and exuded an air of serenity and calmness. Almost saintly. She always had a smile. There wasn't even a hint of one now. She tried to hold back her frustration and burgeoning anger as she continued. Her jaw tightened.

"Dr. Kamen," she said, regaining some of her coolness. "Dr. Kamen, why don't we start with Mrs. Shapiro and Mrs. Fox. You know who they are, don't you? And you know who their husbands are, don't you? You know their husbands are members of our Board, don't you?"

"Uh, well, yes...I do know and I admit Sister that what happened and what I did was in bad taste. In very bad taste. I shouldn't have done it or said it and I..."

"I think I know what happened," she interrupted. "But I want hear the story from you."

"You're sure? Because I already admit that it was in very poor taste and I am sorry..."

"Tell the story."

"Well, OK," I said. "Well, as you know, the nursery badly needs an intensive care incubatorI've applied for it, and I've even talked to you about it. Remember, it was you that suggested that this could be a non-budgeted item...that it may be an ideal piece of equipment for the Ladies Auxiliary to purchase from their raffles and gift shop and..."

"Yes, yes, I know what I said. Please...a little shorter."

"Well, OK, I'm just trying to explain. Well, I contacted Mrs. Hanley, the head Pink Lady and explained everything and told her what you said and she said, 'Fine, if you can sell it to the Volunteer Board, we'll do it.' She was very nice about it."

"Yes, Dr. Kamen, she is very nice, but then you had to go ahead and ruin it, didn't you?"

"First of all, Sister, I admitted what I did was awful, and second of all it finally worked out alright."

"No thanks to you, but I'll tell you about that later. Now, tell me exactly what happened."

"Well, what happened was they asked me to give a talk to the Ladies Auxiliary Board explaining why it was urgent to get the incubator. And I did."

"Yes, you sure did, didn't you? You couldn't, as they say, play it straight, could you? You just had to throw in a funny line, didn't you?"

"Look Sister, I already told you..."

"Alright, alright. What happened?"

"Well, there were about twenty-five women at the meeting. They were all there very well dressed and all...you know...very proper. Nice group. And the talk went very well I think."

"Not at the end it didn't. From what I hear, of course. But go on."

"Yes, well that's when things started to go bad. It was during the question and answer period you know. I had explained how important it was to have the baby in a protected environment, and why it was so important that it should stay warm and receive the right amount of oxygen. Well, as you may have heard, the first question one of the nice ladies asked me was, 'What happens to the baby if it doesn't get enough oxygen?' A pretty basic question, you know."

"I know. Indeed I know."

"Well that's when it happened. I said that if the lack of sufficient oxygen lasted long enough, it could become brain damaged and Lord knows we don't need brain dead people walking around. We already have more than enough politicians."

There was a most uncomfortable silence with neither of us saying anything.

"Dr. Kamen," she began at long last. "When did you get the first inkling that you may have said something...uh...something, shall we say...amiss?"

"Well, when hardly anyone laughed. There were a few titters across the room, but basically, hardly anyone laughed."

"I see. And when were you SURE that something was really wrong?"

"Look, I told you. I did something lousy, but to answer your question, I knew it was all over when Mrs. Hanley introduced me to these two women. They weren't smiling. She said, 'Dr. Kamen, I'd like for you to meet Mrs. Fox and Mrs. Shapiro.' I became mute. I looked first at Mrs. Fox and asked if she would by any chance be related to our mayor...Mayor Fox." I was told yes, that she was his wife."

I shudder at the memory.

"That really stopped me." I continued. "Then Mrs. Fox told me that Mrs. Shapiro was the wife of Stanley Shapiro, the City Attorney."

I knew Stan very well. He and I served for a couple of years on the antipollution board. But I had never met his wife.

"Well, that ended that Sister," I said. "Listen, I apologized ten times over. I apologized. What more could I have done?"

"You could have tried restraining yourself in the first place. Do you know that I got a call from the Mayor that night? Even though he doesn't come to many of the board meetings, he can still be very, very helpful. I need him on our side, Dr. Kamen. Do you understand that?"

I nodded, and said nothing. After a short pause, she began again.

"Now, Dr. Kamen, what about Mr. Douglas and abortion?"

"Oh my gosh...how in heaven's name...how did you hear about that?" I was struck.

"HEAR about it? He's on the governing board. He brought it up at the board meeting, that's how! He read your letter to the entire board."

"But I didn't write that letter to him! " I protested. "I wrote it to General Motors. To the Chevy Division."

"I know, Dr. Kamen, And they sent it to him and he read it to us. He read it and then he gave it to me. Let me read it to you in case you forgot just what you wrote."

"Oh, well that's OK, Sister, I remember what I wrote."

"Well then, I'll just refresh your memory." She began to read from the letter addressed to Donald Branigan, President of the Chevrolet Division of General Motors.

Dear Sir,

I have a question to ask you but first, some background.

I purchased a Chevrolet Sedan from your local dealer, Douglas Chevrolet Motors. I won't bore you with a litany of its defects for you have undoubtedly heard similar complaints. Let me simply mention the highlights.

1. When I pulled out of the agency and stepped on the brake, the car veered sharply to the left. Luckily I was able to retrieve my just traded-in car and two days later, I was told by Mike, the chief mechanic that, "Ha,ha...they forgot one of the discs on the brake."

2. I picked up the car the next day and again pulled out of the dealership. This time, it went two blocks and died completely. It was towed back to the agency and a week later I was told, "Ha, ha...it was a main rod that flipped and we had to replace it."

3. A week after again receiving the car, the weather turned suddenly hot. I turned on the air conditioner. It got hotter. Back to the agency I went and was told, "Ha, ha...nothing is wrong with the air conditioner. Just a mix-up in the switches."

4. I'll skip the next few catastrophes but will mention just one more that I will forever remember. I was driving along the expressway when I heard a thump coming from the back. I glanced back and noticed that the back of the seat had fallen off. I continued home and called the service department. Mike came to the phone. I told him that the back seat fell off. He told me to hold on, he's going to put Mr. Douglas himself on the phone. You won't believe what Mr. Douglas asked me. He asked how it was that I knew the back seat had fallen off. I was stunned. I managed to control myself and finally was able to tell him that I heard a thump, turned around and saw a big hole and wondered what it was that was originally in that hole and then I came up with the idea that it could have been a back seat and so I looked down and voila! There it was! I was told by Mr. Douglas that "Ha ha...it's just some welds..."

My question to you then is this, Mr. Branigan: How could anything be born with so many congenital defects? And I'll ask you another question, Mr. Branigan: Have you or your *inspectors ever considered aborting such a car while it is still on your assembly line to prevent misery to itself and its adoptive parent?*

Yours Truly,

Dr. Jack Kamen

There was another protracted pause. Finally, she spoke.

"Dr. Kamen, may I remind you that in a Catholic hospital we do not EVER speak of abortion...not ever...not even in jest."

With that she quickly turned away from me. But it was too late. I had already seen a smile flicker on her face, and she knew I had seen it. She turned back and let the smile bloom broadly.

"Alright, I'll admit it, Dr. Kamen." she said, still grinning. "I think it was a very good letter, but..." She resumed a stern countenance. "But Mr. Douglas didn't think so and Mr. Douglas is the hospital board chairman."

"Sister, believe me, I really had no idea the letter would be sent to him. Believe me!"

She smiled again.

"I believe you. By the way, did they fix your car?"

"No. They had to give me a new one."

"Good. Good for you. But there's still another matter to be taken up here, Dr. Kamen. It's about Mr. Lackley, the board secretary. He said you insulted his daughter but he wouldn't tell me how. He just said it was inexcusable and that you were insufferable. Would you like to tell me about that?"

"Mr. Lackley...Mr. Lackley." I repeated. "You know, I don't even think I know his daughter."

"Well, she isn't a Lackley anymore. She's a nurse on ICU...Susan Remington."

I felt the blood draining from my face.

"You look rather pale, Dr. Kamen."

"Oh my gosh, Sister. Oh my gosh. Mrs. Remington is Lackley's daughter?!! His daughter?!!!"

Sister Anna Theresa nodded.

"Oh my gosh! Oh my gosh!" I was struck.

"Would you stop that and just tell me what happened Dr. Kamen?" she insisted.

"Uh, Sister, forgive me but I really can't...really...uh, this just isn't for a nun's ears. But one thing I'll admit: It was really stupid on my part, and I apologized to her two or three times. The whole thing was really dumb of me. Really dumb."

"Dr. Kamen, I don't care what it is. I want to hear the whole thing, and I promise you I won't be shocked."

"Are you insisting on this?'"

"I am."

"Alright, but this makes me very uneasy." I began. "Well you know I give these ICU courses to the unit nurses every Wednesday morning. Well, two or three weeks ago I talked about central venous catheters, how they are inserted and what they indicate from a physiological standpoint."

"Yes Dr. Kamen. Those lectures are much appreciated. The nurses love them."

"Yes, well thanks. But anyway, getting back to the lecture...I asked the nurses afterwards if they had any questions and Susan put her hand up."

"Susan Remington?"

"That's right. She just came over from Methodist a couple of months ago."

"Yes, go on," she said, tapping her foot.

"I asked her what her question was and she said she didn't have a question, but she did have a comment. Her comment was that she didn't 'like it.' I was, of course, surprised and puzzled by her comment so I asked her what she meant by saying she didn't 'like it.' She said she didn't mean anything in particular, just that she didn't 'like it'.' "

"Alright, so then?"

"So I asked her, 'You mean you don't like it simply because it's new?' She said yes, that because it was a new procedure, she didn't like it. That's when I said that she must have had a horrible wedding night."

Sister Anna Theresa stopped tapping her foot. She suddenly turned away from me again. She tried to control herself, but couldn't and reached for a tissue on the desk to dab her eyes that were tearing from the laughter.

"And then what happened?" she asked, still trying to stifle her laughter.

"Well, then everything broke loose in there. Some of the nurses said that it wasn't that "new" on Susan's wedding night...and, well, you can imagine the rest, Sister."

Sister Anna Theresa was now laughing uncontrollably. I continued.

"Then Susan ran out of the room crying. I ran after her and when I caught up with her I begged her to forgive me. I told her that what I said was lousy and insensitive. And I really thought she had forgiven me because she started to smile and even admitted it was kind of funny. But I guess when she got to thinking about it, she really wasn't amused at all."

"No, I guess not," said Sister Anna Theresa, calming down now. "Her father is still raving mad."

We just sat there for a few moments staring at each other. I smiled. She smiled back.

"So what did the board decide, Sister?" I asked.

She looked at me with the kindness for which I'll always remember her.

"Well, Dr. Kamen, they discussed your future with this institution for a long, long time. It was probably Dr. Bradbury that saved you though. (Dr. Bradbury, as President of the Medical Staff, was automatically a board member during his term of office.) He said you were indispensable to this hospital. Indispensable. And you know, Dr. Kamen," she said, touching my hand ever so gently. "I agreed with him." She seemed to catch herself and then with a certain harshness continued; "A mite crazy, but indispensable. They finally agreed. So the answer to your question Dr. Kamen is that nothing has changed."

I thanked her and left the office to make rounds.

EPILOGUE

Dr. Bradbury was probably repaying me for something that happened several months before. It was when I made a house call on one of Fat Sadie's prostitutes. As I was leaving her room, Dr.

Bradbury emerged in the hall from an opposite door. He had no doctor's bag. He looked startled

"Uh, Jack...uh, Jack," he muttered. "I'll bet you're wondering what I'm doing here."

"No, Tom, I'm not," I said. "Because I haven't seen you here."

"Thanks Jack. I'll remember this."

JEMELIO MELENDES, M.D.

Six years sped by since my arrival at Indiana Harbor Clinic. My practice had grown significantly—grown to the point that the quality of care was less than desired. I estimated that I was treating 90 patients a day. Attempts were made to limit new patients but all ended in failure. Patients would just appear in the office without appointments and would volunteer to wait indefinitely until they could be seen. Often, a patient would call and ask "as a special favor" for me to treat a friend, a relative, a fellow worker, a member of the church, etc.

I found that saying "no" to these people was difficult. That was probably because my ego, which was subject to the normal vicissitudes and disappointments of everyday medical practice, was assuaged by the outpouring. It's also possible that I felt I was doing something worthwhile by proffering decent medical care. That was enough to keep me at the office well into nighttime hours.

Eventually however, the deterioration in the quality of care that normally follows became noticeable to me. My reading time had declined. I attended fewer postgraduate courses and most of all, I was occasionally irritable when hearing minor complaints.

But it was when Shirley pointed out that I was becoming short both to her and to the children that I decided that the time had come to change. I thought about ways to decrease my workload, but had no managerial skills outside of the hospital and was not disciplined sufficiently to pare my practice. My only alternative was to quit family practice and enter a different field.

First, I had to find a residency program in a field that I chose. Then, essentially, abandon general practice.

The nearest hospital offering residency programs was the University of Chicago. Dean Adams headed both the school and the residency program. I secured an early appointment for an interview. It quickly turned sour.

Dean Adams' office was a large walnut paneled, formal room. Dean Adams was a man of the old school: Very proper and formal.

Following the usual and perfunctory introductions, he immediately asked me the all-important question: "What specialty field has your interest, Doctor?"

Astoundingly, I hadn't given much thought to that. My one notion—quitting— left no room for other considerations. As soon as the question was asked, I realized how totally untenable was my status as a seeker of a residency program had become. Had any other applicant ever applied for a residency without knowing what specialty he or she wanted, or at least what he or she was interested in? I stared at Dean Adams unable to speak.

"Well, Dr. Kamen?" he asked again. "What field interests you?"

I hesitated a bit more but found my voice.

"Well, uh, you see Dr. Adams, uh...this is February and of course, most residencies don't begin until July, and, uh...I, of course don't expect an exception to be made in my case so I'll be happy to take anything that is available now."

He was startled. "Anything? Well, Dr. Kamen. Do you mean to tell me that you don't CARE what specialty you wish to eventually spend your life pursuing? You're not saying you really don't care, are you?"

"You see, Dr. Adams, I just thought that..."

I wasn't allowed to finish.

Dr. Adams rose abruptly from his leather desk chair and riveted his eyes on mine.

"That's quite alright Dr. Kamen. K-A-M-E-N, isn't it? Yes. It's quite alright. Just leave your name and phone number with Mrs. Andrews and we'll call if appropriate."

"You see, Dr. Adams..."

"Good day, Dr. Kamen."

I got up and slowly left Dean Adams' office. I meandered into the secretary's office, scribbled my name and phone number on a paper scrap and left.

I walked through the parking lot to get my car. Damn. A lousy two-minute interview, and a catastrophic two-minutes at that. I thought of my office, filled with patients and I imagined myself there for all eternity. I wasted my opportunity. There would be no second chances—at least not with Dean Adams at the University of Chicago.

Shirley was her usual cheerful self as I arrived home an hour later.

"How'd it go?" she asked.

"Uh, nothing's open," I said, not wanting to go over the details of the afternoon.

She looked disappointed.

"Uh, by the way, what field did you tell them you were looking for?"

"What field?" This was more than coincidence, wasn't it?

"Yeah, you know, what field? What specialty do you like?"

"What do you mean, 'what field—what specialty'?"

"What's wrong with you, Jack? You HAVE been thinking about it, haven't you?"

"Of course I have."

"Well then?"

"Well what?"

"Please, Yankel, don't play games. If you don't want to tell me then don't. I don't care."

Now her anger was visible.

"Sher...of course I know what specialty I want. It's just that, uh, right now I'm pretty undecided."

"OK, so what are your main choices?"

"Let's see. There's internal medicine...or OB/GYN and there's Pediatrics...no skip Pediatrics...and there's..."

"Wait. What fields DON'T you like besides Pediatrics?" Shirley asked.

"Well, I don't like dermatology or pathology or anesthesiology. Especially anesthesiology."

"Why especially anesthesiology?"

"Well, can you imagine me sitting at the head of an operating room table for hours and hours while somebody else operates and I'm doing something that a nurse can do just as well. And I'd be beholden to others for cases to do and..."

She stopped me with a raised hand. "Well, Yankele, that's very interesting."

"Why is it so interesting?"

"Because just before you came home, the University of Chicago called and said that the new chairman of the Anesthesia Department had arrived and he'd like for you to stop in tomorrow to talk to him."

I stood there stunned.

"I'm not doing it," I said, defiantly.

"Oh yes you are!" Shirley snapped. "I made the appointment and you'll be there tomorrow at 2 in his office!"

"I'm not going into anesthesia!"

"Two P.M.!"

"I'm not going!"

"Room 560. Old Building."

"I'm not..."

"Tomorrow at 2!"

•••••••••••••••••••

I started my anesthesia residency six weeks after the interview with Dean Adams, under the aegis of Dr. Duncan Holiday, the new Anesthesia Department Chairman. He was—and is— the paragon of teachers. He was able to correct almost immediately my misconceptions about the field of anesthesia. By the time my two year stint was completed, my perception was that an anesthesiologist had to be the most astute of all physicians, especially in the areas of physiology, pharmacology and anatomy. It was also because of his teaching skills that I became interested in intensive care and respiratory therapy. Ultimately, after a research fellowship, I became the Chairman of these departments at St. Mary Mercy Hospitals in Gary and Hobart, Indiana.

Dr. Holiday accepted me into the anesthesia residency. True, he had to overcome some misgivings raised by Dean Adams, but overall, this wasn't too difficult. But when I came home from the University of Chicago that day, I was really depressed. My entire professional world seemed to be collapsing. Misgiving piled on doubts which mingled with sadness at the thought of leaving all my patients. I was certain that they couldn't survive without my medical ministerings. How wrong I was.

I was imagining horsedrawn carts plodding through the streets, picking up corpses from each home—as during the Black Plague of the Middle Ages. (It was a bit jolting to realize that after I had been gone for several months, all my patients were doing quite nicely. So much for indispensability.

Immediately after announcing my departure date to my office personnel, I got down to the task of finding my replacement. The name of the perfect doctor came quickly.

Jemelio Melendez had completed his internship eight months before and was working on a part-time basis in a local clinic. Of first generation Spanish descent, he was born six blocks from my office in a home in which his mother and father and three of their eight children still resided. His parents and three other siblings made many sacrifices to put him through medical school and he was anxious to repay them. "Jimmy" spent two months with me during his senior elective, and I was very impressed with his acumen and willingness to put in long hours. His ability to speak Spanish in a largely Spanish-speaking neighborhood added to his invaluable assets. He had a single flaw, which I thought minor.

Jimmy was handsome; the epitome of the Latin lover. His demeanor bordered on shyness, but this only added to his "Romeo-like" image. My office nurses, both married, carried on like giggly adolescents when he was near. My receptionist and secretary would stare at him when he was close by. More darkly, however, he seduced a young woman—while she was babysitting for Shirley and me at our home— by promising her marriage, even though he was engaged at the time to a Spanish girl who he subsequently married of necessity three months later. He was handsome...and he knew it.

Even though I had some qualms about his behavior, I offered him my practice and he accepted. During the ensuing five weeks, I introduced him to my patients, most of whom readily accepted the idea that he would be seeing them in my stead. At the end of the sixth week, after a tearful farewell party, I left for my new residency.

I remained in touch with my former office personnel. He had retained all of them except for the receptionist who left to return to school. He replaced her with one of his sisters who later also became his business manager. All reports by the office staff were enthusiastic. He was a hard worker, compassionate, and most of all, he was knowledgeable.

All was well...perfect, in fact...until I received a call from a former patient four months after I left. It was after dinner.

"Dr. Kamen? This is Alice Dunigan. Do you remember me?"

"Of course, Mrs. Dunigan. How are you? And how's Big Jim and Junior?"

"Oh we're all OK, but I am calling about a serious problem."

"Oh?"

"Oh no, it's not an illness or anything like that. But it's about your replacement, Dr. Melendes."

"Yes?"

224

"You see, Dr. Kamen. Well, uh...I'll uh get right to the point." She hesitated only for a second. "He raped me."

"He...he...he WHAT?"

"Yes, Dr. Kamen, he raped me and it's been on my mind ever since it happened, and I just had to tell somebody and so I thought you should know."

"He raped you? He actually raped you?"

"Yes, and I don't know what to do about it. I thought it best to call you."

"Well, Mrs. Dunigan, you know of course that this is a criminal offense."

"I know it is."

"Uh, if you care to, why don't you tell me exactly what happened. When did this occur?

"About two weeks ago."

"Two weeks ago?" I had unintentionally raised my voice. It must have made me sound perplexed.

"Well yes, but it's been on my mind ever since."

"Yes, I can imagine. Go on."

"Well, about two weeks ago like I said, Jim Junior was running a high fever and vomiting. He's only six months old, you know. You delivered him."

"Yes, I remember."

"Well I called Dr. Melendes to come over to the house to check Junior and he got here in about a half an hour.

"What time of day was it?"

"Oh, I guess it was about one o'clock in the afternoon. My husband was at work at the time you know."

"Yes."

"Yes, well he finished examining the baby and told me Junior had an ear infection. Then he gave the baby a shot."

"Yes?"

"So then he went out of the bedroom and into the living room, and we just started talking and..."

"Talking about what?" I interrupted.

"Oh just about everything and nothing in particular. And then he asked me if I got along well with my husband and I said that I did pretty well. Then he asked me if my husband was gentle with me and I asked him what he meant, and he said, 'you know, does he really treat you right when he's making love to you'...and I said, 'I guess so' and before I knew it, he was unbuttoning my blouse."

"Uh, Mrs. Dunigan, at that time...right at that point, did you ask him to stop? Did you ask him not to do that?"

"Of course not!"

"Of course not? Why not?!!"

"Why not? Well, I didn't want to wake up the baby by making a fuss."

"You didn't want to wake the baby?"

"Of course. Dr. Kamen, this was the first time in hours that he wasn't crying. So I wouldn't dare make any noise that would wake him."

"Couldn't you have just whispered to him...to Dr. Melendez...that you weren't interested and to stop?" I asked.

226

"Well, I didn't think of it at the time. But anyway, who knows what might have happened?"

"And then what?"

"Well, that's about it. We had sex on the floor."

"Mrs. Dunigan, did you yourself take any of your own clothes off?"

"Uh, well...uh...I guess I did. He didn't know how my bra fastened in the back."

"Mrs. Dunigan, were you a willing partner?"

"No, not really. I really didn't think I wanted to have sex with him. Not really."

I paused. "Well, Mrs. Dunigan, it is of course your right to press charges if that's what you want to do. I'm no lawyer of course, but I have my doubts about whether you'd be successful."

"You're probably right, Dr. Kamen, and of course I wouldn't want Jim to know, but I had to tell somebody, and I guess I just wanted you to know what a horrible doctor you got to replace you."

I wished her well and hung up.

Her accusations seemed to be ludicrous when she called me again about a week later telling me that Dr. Melendez had done it again. She told me she had called him to come to the house to check on Junior again. This time, he took off her bra, having quickly mastered the undoing of the snaps after their last rendezvous.

EPILOGUE

Dr. Melendez, from several other reports I received, was becoming well-known for his frequent sexual romps with young, attractive female patients. His reputation as an outstanding medical practitioner remained unscathed.

Sadly, however, Dr. Melendez suffered a massive myocardial infarction (heart attack) during one of his extramarital couplings. He was forced to abandon the booming practice after only four years, and acquire a position that would produce much less strain and tension.

He became the physician for several area nursing homes, where his practice was limited to the elderly and patients with disabilities.

MRS. SOPHIA MURPHY

She never lost her heavy Greek accent. To the contrary, she appeared to flaunt it, to revel in it. Her,"I know some English good, ask me," sounded like. "I noosome Anglish goot-acks me." But then, in her social life, she associated exclusively with her own country people. Only Hellenic people. Her church was, of course, Greek Orthodox. The restaurants patronized were all Greek cuisine and/or Greek owned and operated. Her shopping trips were to Chicago's "Greek Town." In these places, Mrs. Murphy...Mrs. Sophia Murphy...was in her natural environment. Of course this was not Mr. Murphy's milieu, but he didn't care. Though married to his war bride for twelve years, he never attempted to learn even a few rudimentary Greek words. Nothing. He knew "Baklava" and "Uzu" (a Greek liqueur.) He knew "Shishkabob"— but beyond that, the language was really just Greek. Why did he need to know it anyway? He loved Sophia and what English she knew was enough. He owned a very successful trucking business, and "I don't ship crates to Crete," as he was fond of telling everyone. So, Mr. Murphy and Sophia were happy. An unlikely couple...but an idyllic marriage. Everything was perfect, except...

I got the late evening call at home. As soon as I heard the caller's voice, I knew it was Sophia. She had been my patient for a long time at the Indiana Harbor Clinic before she and her husband moved to Michigan City, Indiana. Still, the voice was unmistakable—somewhat unintelligible—but telltale with the heavy Greek accent.

"Docta!" she began. "I hate bother you but no want call office. I need time talk to you private."

"Sure, Mrs. Murphy," I said. "Tell you what. Why don't you come in tomorrow at eight in the morning. I'll have at least a half an hour before anyone else arrives."

"No, I want talk now. Private."

"Yes, well, we're on the phone, so it is private Mrs. Murphy."

"Nobody listen?"

"No, Mrs. Murphy."

"Alright. You sure nobody listen?"

"Yes, I'm sure."

"Alright. Now I tell you. I want you should do a blow job on me. A good job. Two or three times. My husband rich. He pay anything...any money. I come in tomorrow, eight o'clock. You do me blow job then."

"Just a minute here, Mrs. Murphy. Just wait. What exactly did you just say?"

Her accent was getting worse. She undoubtedly meant something else. But what? WHAT something else? Blood? Did she want a "blood job"? Flow? A flow job? No. Below job? Nope. Or maybe...

"OK, now Mrs. Murphy. Say it again, but this time, say it as slowly as you can."

"Wait, Docta Kamen. Wait. I put my husband to phone. You wait."

I waited.

"Look, Doc..." said John (Big Red) Murphy. "I know what's going on in your head right now, and it sounds awful, but that's what her sister called it. She called it a blow job."

"Her sister? Who's her sister?"

"Helena. You know Helena Phulhausen?"

"Helena is Sophia's sister?"

"Sure, Doc. You didn't know?"
230

"But Helena has no ..."

"I know she has no accent Doc. Helena was here before Sophia was even born. She married a Dutch freighter Captain and they settled in Connecticut. Then they both came to Indiana after the war so she could look after her little sister. Of course, this was after her husband retired."

"So Helena is Sophia's sister."

"Sure enough, Doc. And Helena called and told Sophia what you did to her was a blow job."

All was now clear.

Having no children, being barren, was a horrible stigma for a Greek woman to bear, just as it is for many others. It was not only the woman that suffered, but also her husband, perhaps even more than the woman. He would perceive himself as having a lesser masculinity. His wife shared his agony for she always considered her barrenness her "fault."

"John," I said, "I understand what you mean now, but you know, we don't call it a blow job."

"Doc, I know it isn't what it is in the street, but she told me and Sophia that you did blow her up and...uh...I mean, that's what she said. And I asked her if you used a straw or something and then she told me about the explosion and everything.

"Now wait, John," I interjected. "Look. Let me start at the beginning here. First, it wasn't an 'explosion,' it was...uh...wait. Let me explain what it is and as long as Helena already told you, I can tell you what happened. Because it wasn't exactly an explosion."

"Go ahead, Doc. I'll listen. But Sophia wants the same blow...I mean...uh...treatment."

"OK John, look. First, it's called a 'tubal insufflation.' "

"Inflation? You mean like a balloon? I mean, that IS blowing into it...isn't it?"

"No, no John. Not inflation...INSUFFLATION. Look, you know Helena came to see me because she couldn't have children."

"Sure Doc. That's what we're talking about."

"Alright. So one of the things we do is make sure the passageway from the ovaries to the inside of the womb is open so the egg can get in the womb and the sperm..."

"Wait Doc. Just a minute. Are you telling me that women—human women—lay eggs?"

"John, hold on. First let me get through telling you what happened and then I'll explain some of the facts of reproduction. Women do make eggs, but not like a chicken egg with a shell and everything, but it's still an egg—a very tiny egg about the size of a dot. But that's getting off the subject. Let me start again. When a woman makes an egg, it goes into her belly and then down a tube where the baby will begin, but that's where it needs to meet a sperm."

"I know how the sperm gets there." offered John. "It has to go up a tube and..."

"Right. Let me finish." I continued, "If the sperm meets the egg in the womb, a baby can start. OK?"

"Sure."

"OK. Now one of the things we do is make certain that the tube is open for the egg to travel through to the womb. To do that, we blow—I mean, uh—we insufflate—-uh, that is—we push a gas through the tubes."

"OK, I'm with you."

"Good. Now the way we do this is we put a metal tube into the cervix. This is the opening of the womb."

"Like a straw."

"Well no—well, yes—-I guess it's like a very small metal straw."

"Like I said, Doc."

"Right. OK. Now wait. Let me finish. We hook this tube to carbon dioxide."

"Hey, we haul a lot of that stuff Doc. They make soda out of it."

"That's right. Exactly. In fact, what we do is take a small cartridge filled with carbon dioxide—you know the same that's used in a seltzer bottle—and we take this cartridge and put it into this gizmo that looks like an cannon shell, and we screw the top of this gizmo down until the cartridge is punctured by a hollow spike. This releases the gas that I can control with a small valve."

"So it's like a little bomb or grenade?"

"Well, I guess it's something like that."

"Well, then how did it explode? Helena told me that you put this, this...well...straw into her, her..."

"Cervix."

"No she didn't say that cervix word. She said you put it into her..."

"Whatever."

"Yeah, whatever. Well, she said that then you turned on a switch and then it exploded and this bomb went off and shot across the room like a rocket — and she jumped off the table and tried to run, but all this metal junk was hanging out of her, uh..."

"Vagina."

"Yeah, whatever. And that you were hollering, and the nurse was hollering and she was screaming she was shot and the two of you held her and..."

"Yes. Let me just say that —well, that was rather unfortunate."

"I'll bet it was."

"Uh, yes. You see, I didn't screw the cover on tightly enough and when the gas was released, well, it did shoot through the room like a rocket."

"Yeah, well Doc it really scared the hell out of her. She told Sophia she had diarrhea for two days."

"Yes. Like I said, it was rather unfortunate."

"Yeah, and now she says she doesn't even know how you got her back on the table with her legs up so that you could try again."

"You might say it took some persuasion."

"I'll bet. Well anyway, she's pregnant. I mean she's good and pregnant. I mean, here she is now, forty-two years old and she's all over the place showing off her belly all over Greek town, all over church and everything."

"I have to admit to you John that I told Helena that insufflation probably wouldn't help her, because she was about past the childbearing age. I went so far as to tell her I thought it had no chance at all of working for her and that the whole thing was pretty much a waste of time. Luckily, I was wrong."

"Yeah, you were wrong, but it worked on her girlfriend too, because she and Helena are out there comparing bellies. And Doc, Sophia wants this too. She wants to be, like you said, insufferated."

234

"Insufflated."

"Right. And I want it too, Doc. We both want it real bad."

Before I hung up with John and Sophia, I made an appointment for them to come to the office the next day for the treatment. Everything proceeded smoothly, with no unscheduled liftoffs, explosions, or detonations.

EPILOGUE

Sophia and John conceived a child three months later, but Sophia miscarried the baby in her third month. One year later, they conceived again, and she gave birth to a healthy baby girl. Then the next year, John Murphy Junior entered the world weighing in at 9 lbs.10 oz.

Following the birth of their first child, John Murphy Sr. sent me a large truck model with his company's logo on it. Inside was a single bottle of seltzer water and a straw.

MANNY ROMULA

Whenever a male gypsy was admitted to a hospital, he and his family and friends would immediately proclaim him as "King of the Gypsies."

"He king of all Gypsies!" they would exclaim. "ALL Gypsies! He King of all Gypsy kings!"

This litany of their loved one's absolute royalty was familiar, so upon Mr. Romula's admittance to our intensive care unit, we were admonished by his entourage to treat him with the utmost care and respect, as a great king deserves.

But King Romula and his subjects did not appear to be blue-blooded. There was no evidence of the demeanor usually associated with aristocracy. The assemblage of his cousins, brothers, and even his wife...about ten...all disheveled and distraught, followed the king's stretcher into the unit, even bolting past two security guards whose job was to initially restrict visitors. His cousin, particularly menacing, issued a warning to all in a hoarse, threatening voice; "He's the big one! The big king! The big, big king! Better take good, good care! All of you hear? Take good, good care. I be watching."

His Highness, however, was unable to speak. There was a plastic tube in his trachea (windpipe), that had been inserted through an incision in his neck by the Emergency Room physician, who had correctly surmised that the King would need long-term breathing assistance. All of his breathing was through this tube. No air went through his vocal cords, so speech was impossible. However, he was alert enough to briskly touch his chest with his forefinger whenever the word "King" was uttered. Even this small movement must have caused him acute pain, for his chest had multiple rib fractures.

236

And then there were the curses. A chorus of curses. They came down in incantations, intonations of magic, holy curses—a cacophony of epithets. The curses were intoned mostly against one soul, and one soul only...that of Lou Bostick.

How unfair! Their predicament was surely fate's cruelty... a senseless, needless, ferocious strike against this hysterical liege.

Earlier that day, King Romula was working with his Uncle Mike, running a "tree-trimming" scam, as they did every day. No problems. The first homeowner was angry and upset, threatening to sue and everything. All was normal. No problems.

The con Manny and Mike were running was simple. Manny and Mike would cruise a better than average neighborhood until they spotted a home with tree branches overhanging a roof or pushing against a porch. Even decaying or dead branches would do nicely. Then Manny would go to the door and ring the bell, introduce himself, and make the unsuspecting homeowner a deal they would find irresistible.

"Good morning Meester. You see there? You see this tree branch on your roof? Soon will damage roof and then you got big problems. I tell you what. I cut branches for you...only five dollars for each branch. Only five dollars! But only today. Right now. We in neighborhood only today and want to make little money for us...not give to boss. Boss own everything."

Naturally, this "only happens once" deal made some trusting residents agreeable to Manny's proposal. After all, wouldn't you rather pay five bucks now to remove a hanging dead branch rather than hundreds of dollars later to repair an entire roof? Before they could even finish shaking their heads yes, the chain saw was out and the cutting began. Then in a half an hour, with mission accomplished, Manny would return to the door to summon the homeowner for payment.

"All done now Meester! Let's see." Manny would say as he wrote some figures on a dirty scratch pad. "That be six-hundred dollars.".

"But you said only five dollars a branch! There were only two or three branches!"

"No, no, no, no!" Manny would say, shaking his head and smiling. "No, not two branches...120 branches! See?"

And with that, Manny would hold up a 6"-8" piece of the tree. Granted, it was small, but technically, it was still a branch.

"See? We no lie! We count 120 branches!"

Typically, there would then be raucous arguing."But...but...but...I thought...uh...I didn't think..." Then, when the shock wore off and all became clear, the next sentence would be more easily understood.

"Get out of here, or I'm calling the police! Then I'm calling the Better Business Bureau! Then I'm calling..."

"Meester, Meester," Manny would interrupt while mustering a look of deep understanding and compassion. "Meester, alright, look. Maybe you don't understand. Look, I see, you don't understand what I say to you before I do work for you. Look, alright, I don't want no trouble."

Manny would then pull out the small dirt stained scratch pad and pencil stub from his pocket and busily scribble, then scratch, then scribble again. Meanwhile, during this process, he would look up at the homeowner a couple of times with puzzled and innocent eyes.

"Look, I spleet with you. I no want you be mad about thees. I spleet even. Feefty-feefty. You give me $200 and I go. But cash. Cash only."

The homeowner would be glad the man couldn't divide, and would likely get the money to Manny right away. Then Manny would be gone before the homeowner realized his mistake. Done.

Easy. Street to street, every day, they'd run their scam. They'd succeed at least ten times a day. The money was great and it was easy.

Easy. Until Lou Bostick.

Manny didn't know his name when he first went up to the door and knocked. No, it was just another job. And it started off well enough. All seemed to be well on track with Lou Bostick...just another job.

Lou was a big man. A very big man. Manny was no shrimp, but Lou was much bigger than Manny. Much bigger. About 55 years old, Lou was a construction foreman, but now, Manny found him home, between jobs. Lou agreed to Manny's branch cutting proposal, and in a half hour, Manny came back seeking payment, as always.

That's when things started to unravel. Manny's Uncle Mike told me what happened when Lou came to the door, and a tornado sprang up.

"What the shit did you just say?" Lou shouted at Manny.

"I say $600. 120 branches...$600," said Manny. But the intense look of utter rage on Lou's face cut short Manny's act.

"Alright, Meester. I no want make trouble. I spleet with you, feefty-feefty. Give me $200 and everything even." Manny proposed.

"What the shit did you just say?" As he spoke, Lou seemed to become even larger. His chest heaved up. His face turned crimson-scarlet. The veins in his neck bulged.

"Alright Meester, alright. I take feefty dollars then I go. Feefty dollars then everything even."

Lou took a step forward. Manny whirled and ran—sprinted—toward his pickup truck parked on the street. He fled. He was hollering in a jumbled combination of Romanian and English.

"Mike! Get into truck! Mike! Fast! Mike!"

Mike, having observed Big Lou and the proceedings at Lou's front door, had no trouble assessing the predicament. Lou was in hot pursuit of Manny, and was only about ten feet behind him, his savagery still evident. Manny continued to scream. Mike hurled the chainsaw into the pickup bed and dived into the cab. Manny ran for the driver's side. Lou went for the chainsaw.

Lou picked it up, waved it over his head, lowered it, and with one great pull, brought it buzzing to life. The battered Chevy 260 started to pull away. But Lou, in his white-hot hate, swung at the spinning tires and hit, shredding the tire and tearing the chainsaw from his hand. It bounced under the truck which was now careening out of control. In a half block, it suddenly veered and smashed full force into a delivery van, compressing the front end and jamming the steering wheel into Manny's chest. Mike escaped with a small knee laceration.

X-rays showed Manny had numerous rib fractures and multiple lung hemorrhages. This internal bleeding caused the normally spongy lungs to become sodden and heavy. Breathing was labored as Manny tried to breathe with a chest that had multiple rib fractures. His respiratory distress worsened on arrival in the trauma room. He was rapidly intubated— a plastic tube inserted through the mouth into the trachea (windpipe) — and placed on a respirator which did his breathing for him. The tracheostomy followed.

Manny was in the unit for one week on a respirator when an insidious but ominous change occurred. Small traces of blood began to appear in the tracheotomy tube. It was called to my attention by the Chief of Respiratory Therapy who noticed it when an ICU nurse was suctioning secretions from the opening.

"I think he's eroding," he told me.

This was very serious and very disheartening. Tracheal erosion was and is a very dangerous condition. To explain:

Patients undergoing any major surgery will almost always have a plastic tube inserted into their trachea with the protruding end attached to an anesthesia apparatus. The anesthesiologist or the nurse anesthetist would then be able to "breathe" for the patient by either squeezing on a breathing bag or turning on a respirator. Patients who are in respiratory difficulty, such as Manny, have these tubes inserted as lifesaving measures as soon as possible.

In order to make this system airtight, so the oxygen or air will go into the lungs and not escape around the tube and out of the mouth, a seal between the tube and the tracheal wall is needed. This is provided by inflating an inflatable cuff that surrounds the tube near its tracheal tip. This ring, or cuff, is inflated through a smaller tube of its own with small increments of air, until the system is tight. But here lies the problem. Although care is usually taken in expanding the cuff, the actual pressure which the cuff exerts against the delicate airway tissues is difficult to measure, and at times, the force may be excessive. Combined with malnutrition, common in the acutely ill or injured, and long-term placement, (days, weeks, or months instead of hours as in surgery), the airway membrane may become ulcerated or eroded. If erosion continues, the trachea may perforate, either into the esophagus (gullet) which is directly behind it, or into a large artery—two events which carry a fatal prognosis.

Many devices and cuff modifications had appeared, but none proved to be sufficiently successful in reducing the incidence of tracheal erosion.

On hearing the news of Manny's worsening condition, I inspected the suction matter and confirmed that blood was indeed being brought up—the first sign of erosion.

"And to make matters worse," said Mrs. Harrigan the ICU Assistant Head Nurse, "The skin over his sacrum is breaking down and we ran out of sheepskins."

Bedsores. This was a nursing stigma, a sign of inadequate care. But Manny was a prime candidate for bedsores. Lying immobile, attached to a respirator, inadequate protein intake and a firm mattress all contributed to skin erosion or bedsores. Even though he was being turned regularly from side to side, it was not enough. And putting a piece of natural sheepskin with the wool on the sore, usually helped significantly. But now, there were no more in stock.

"I think I'll put a foam rubber pad under him for the time being," said Mrs. Harrigan. She was determined to avoid the stigma.

With much help, a foam pad was taken from the seat of a wheelchair and was placed under Manny's posterior. He sensed relief.

I stared at the pad.

"Wait a minute!" I started. "Why not put this in his trachea?"

"Because it won't fit," offered Mrs. Harrigan.

"No, why not cut a piece and use it instead of the air cuff?"

"Because it'll get soaking wet."

"No, why not put a cover over it and attach the whole thing to the tube? A foam rubber "O" ring."

She didn't respond at first, and then:

"Alright. Why don't you do it?"

I went to Central Supply to get a new tracheostomy tube. I ripped off the air cuff. Then they gave me an old seat cushion and the maintenance department punched out a cylinder of the foam rubber. I put a hole in its center and fitted it on the tube where the air cuff had been. Then I cut off the thumb of a surgical glove and made a covering for the foam which I then glued to the tube. In two hours I was back at Manny's bedside.

"Here it is!" I proclaimed to to the ICU staff. They surrounded the bed.

"Will it work?" asked the respiratory therapist.

"Hell if I know."

Manny's eyes suddenly grew larger. We had forgotten that he could hear and understand us. With false bravado, I reassured him.

"Oh Manny, we're going to fix you up! Now don't worry, really," I gulped.

The air was evacuated from the cuff through the same port that inflated the air ring, causing the foam to collapse, and allowing for easier insertion.

The ties holding Manny's tube in place were released and the old device pulled out. The new tracheotomy tube was swiftly inserted in its place and the foam rubber was allowed to re-expand by allowing the air to go in. He was reconnected to the respirator. Then we waited. The respirator went through three cycles and we all relaxed.

"It works! It works!" from an ICU nurse. "It's airtight and it works!!"

And work it did. The bleeding stopped and in three weeks, Manny was able to breathe on his own. The tube was then removed and a week later, he was discharged from the hospital...ready to go back to "work."

As for the moral question of what I had done...using an untested, makeshift device experimentally in dire circumstances, such as Manny's, was an ethically acceptable practice. But to institute the new tracheal cuff on a general scale required research and clinical trials to accomplish this.

I contacted Dr. Carolyn Wilkinson of Wesley Hospital in Chicago. As a physician who was frustrated by the problems using the standard tracheal cuff, she was excited and positive about this "breakthrough." Her faith in the new device was perhaps even greater than my own. Our investigative work began.

Our first problem was to find the perfect spongy material for the cuff. It needed to be a substance with minimal firmness, or else its bulk would make insertion difficult, in which case an airtight seal might not be possible. Manny's emergency foam cuff worked, but even it was too firm. I assumed the task of finding the right spongy foam for the new cuffs, and I began looking wherever and whenever I could, trying everything—from packaging materials to upholstery to the padding in shoes and children's sponge balls. I tried everything. None seemed to be just right.

It was on the way to a our department store with my wife, Shirley, that I thought of another possibility. Shirley had dragged me along to buy a plastic cover for her new tablecloth. The aisle to "linens" passed through the ladies' lingerie department. A saleslady was there standing present. I approached her.

"Excuse me, Miss," I began.

244

"Yes sir. How can I help you?" asked the fifty-ish, proper looking woman.

"Excuse me, Miss. But could I please see your falsies?"

She slowly backed away. Then she straightened up.

"I beg your pardon, sir!" she said, with the emphasis on "beg."

Shirley, who had been standing a few feet ahead of me, came back to where we were standing. She noticed the look on the dumbstruck woman's face.

"Jack, what did you just ask her for?"

"I just wanted to see her falsies."

Innocent.

"Oh my God, Jack! You asked to see her...her...oh my God!"

"For heaven's sake, Shirley, I just want to see if they're the right..."

"I know...I know what you want them for. But she..."

Shirley turned to the poor saleslady who held the look of reserved indignation on her face. She tried to speak to her, but found it difficult. Finally:

"Ma'am, he just wants to...uh..." She couldn't finish. The saleslady turned to me.

"Alright, sir. Now may I ask what size 'figure enhancers' you are in need of?"

"Yes, of course. I want the biggest size you have. The bigger the better. I just want to feel it."

Shirley's mouth dropped open. She tried to explain again.

"You see, ma'am, he just wants to use them for kind of an experiment."

"I understand, my dear," said the woman. She pitied Shirley. "I understand. I'll be right back." She turned and slowly walked away slowly...very slowly...looking over her shoulder once or twice as she disappeared into the backroom.

"Jack!" Shirley said, her face a dull red. "Do you know what she's thinking? She's thinking you're some kind of pervert. That's what she's thinking. Pervert! Pervert!" Shirley was angry.

"I just want to tell you one thing, Jack. I don't know you, I've never seen you before in my life, and I'm leaving this store now. I'll go to Sears or something, but I know I can never shop in this store again!" She turned and stalked out the door. I told her I'd be there in a minute. She didn't turn around.

Ms. Understanding returned. She was carrying two "full-figured bra inserts," one in each hand. She proffered one to me with a fully outstretched arm. It was apparent that she wanted to keep her distance.

"Well, sir, will these do?"

A preteen girl with her mother stopped to watch us. Then the mother quickly yanked her fascinated child away. Like Shirley, I too was ready for this episode to end. And I was also sure I'd never walk into the store again.

Carefully, I took the pale pink pad and, trying to appear casual and nonchalant, I squeezed it gently. I did not look the saleslady in the eye.

"Oh, uh, I'm sorry Miss," I said. "I'm afraid this is cotton batting...you know it won't collapse...and it's much to difficult to insert...no...no...I need something soft...more like a sponge...something with a softer feel."

I rapidly put the pad back into her hand with a very quick "but thanks for your trouble anyhow." I turned and quickly sprinted out of the store.

Finding the correct foam-like material for the new cuff on the commercial market proved to be difficult. I finally discovered it in the Sears upholstery department. The foam material was eventually manufactured to order by a small plastics firm that made other medical devices. But finding an acceptable rubber sheath to cover the cuff posed no such difficulties. This cuff, at least for research and experimental purposes, could be covered perfectly with an ordinary non-lubricated condom, the closed end cut open.

Joyce, my youngest daughter, who was 15 years old, and Daniel, my youngest son, was eleven years old when the initial research on the cuff began. I enlisted their help in making the new tracheal tubes. I supplied them with all of the materials and I instructed them on how to construct each one. Their payment was 50¢ per cuff, so they were most eager to undertake the task.

On a Sunday, Daniel came into my room where I was reading.

"Hey Dad," he said. "I don't have any more balloons left."

I gave him some money and asked him to go to the drugstore. I also gave him a note asking for a dozen "non-lubricated" condoms. Antony Carducci, the neighborhood pharmacist and a longtime friend, looked at Daniel with some puzzlement as he received my note. He said nothing as he filled the order.

Daniel returned home and he and Joyce began working. Three hours later, he came into my room again.

"Hey Dad," he said. "We got some more done, but I ruined a few of the new balloons so we need more to finish the rest."

I gave him more money, and once again, Daniel sped off on his bike.

"Hi, Mr. Tony! I'm back!" said Daniel. "I need another dozen of what I bought before!"

Antony stared at Daniel...immobile and silent.

"Uh, Dan," he began, coming to the front of the counter, crouching and lowering his voice. "Uh, do you know what these are and what they're used for?" Antony held up a package of Trojans Un-lubricated.

Daniel's eyes lit. A large broad smile beamed across his face. He was prepared to display his brilliance in answering. Other customers and staff looked at him.

"Oh, why sure." said Daniel, smiling and speaking loudly and proudly. "My Dad uses these to put down people's throats. He's doing it all the time now."

There wasn't a sound in the store.

"And," Daniel continued, aware that he now had the rapt attention of others in the small pharmacy. "Not only that, but he teaches other people how to do it too. He says he wants them to do it as well as he does."

Nobody moved.

Antony cleared his throat then rose slowly. He glanced at the other customers in the store who, by this time, had begun whispering to each other about "Dr. Kamen's son." Antony went to the phone.

It took me several minutes to unravel what he was telling me. Then, as I tried to explain what Daniel was doing, I realized it was useless. I got in the car and drove to the pharmacy, bringing one

248

of the tracheal tubes with me. I showed it to Antony, purchased the condoms, and left the store.

Selling the concept of the new endotracheal tube was frustrating. All of the American and Canadian manufacturers were contacted and all showed only tepid interest. It was only after exhausting these possibilities that we contacted foreign firms, and finally got a nibble from a large German corporation. They invited us, (Dr. Carolyn Wilkinson and myself), to Frankfurt to present our new device to their scientists and production personnel. We accepted.

Dr. Wilkinson can best be described as a very outgoing and vivacious person. She was eager to escape from her work schedule to go to Europe to sell the tube. Excited at the prospects of success, we arrived at the airport early.

It was about this time that hijacking and terrorist activities were peaking (1967-68). Weapon detection devices in airports were still in their embryonic stage so personal inspections were still the primary screening techniques. The U.S. Customs service was initially assigned the job of outbound security—a change for them.

We put our bags on the conveyor belt and inched our way to the agent's post. Cases were being randomly checked.

"You know, sir," Carolyn said to the agent. "I think I'd look through this gentleman's belongings." She pointed to me.

My luggage was almost off the belt when he motioned for me to stop and return to the post.

"Please open your bag, sir," said the agent brusquely.

The German company had asked us to bring enough materials to demonstrate how we constructed our tracheal tubes. So I had with me the foam and the "blank tubes"— that is, tubes that do not yet have cuffs applied.

"I'm sorry sir," the agent continued. "But once we have received a request of this sort, I must make a thorough inspection. Open all your bags."

It only took me a brief moment to explain to the agent what the devices were. He looked through a few of them to make certain there were no hidden explosives, and then he closed the case. The line started to move again.

"Uh, excuse me, sir," I said to the agent. "Aren't you going to check HER things?"

Carolyn blushed instantly, then her face became crimson red.

"No, no...that's alright," she said. "It's just more of the same."

"I'm sorry Miss. The request has been made," came the agent's expected reply.

"No, no, really. It's all part of the same things he has."

"Open your bags, Miss."

The other passengers in line were restless. Carolyn opened the lid of her suitcase, and there, on top of all her clothing was a scattered gross of condoms.

"Uh, I see. I see," said the flustered agent.

Carolyn, looking down, found herself unable to respond.

Perfunctorily, the agent shuffled through her clothes, mumbling, "I see, I see." She started to say, "This isn't what you think..." but was stopped.

"No need Ma'am. No need," proclaimed the agent. He closed the suitcase and motioned for us to pass.

Carolyn grabbed the handle of her suitcase, yanked it off the conveyor and walked to the gate. Her face was still the color of a warning beacon. We got on the plane, and took off for Germany.

EPILOGUE

The "Kamen-Wilkinson Endotracheal Tube" was finally manufactured by an American company co-owned by a physician who had given up his practice and by an ex-medical device salesman. Variations of the tube are still in use today worldwide.

Afterword (In my own words)

After speaking on the phone one day in 2010 with my Dad, he asked if I wanted to speak to Mom before we hung up. "Of course," I said, looking forward to hearing her pick up the extension and speak my name as only she can. "Joycie!!! My baby!!!" she always exclaimed, never masking her thrill at the prospect of talking to me. At once, her love poured out of the telephone receiver and filled me completely. My sister and two brothers know exactly what I mean. They got the same greeting with each new phone call, each visit or new encounter. The re-entry of any one of her children into her immediate world (this now includes her sons and daughters-in-law, grandchildren and great-grandchildren) brings her the greatest joy imaginable.

On this particular day, I had been speaking on the phone with my Dad about the collection of short stories we were writing together. I was working on the

stories, adding in more depth in the narrative about the times themselves—and about life in general in Indiana Harbor during that bygone era.

"Mom, I've got Dad's take on some things about those days in Gary," I told her. "But Dad thinks I should ask you about a few things too." She seemed quite surprised that we wanted to include her thoughts and reminiscences in the book.

"You want to ask ME some questions?" she asked, still disbelieving, but definitely eager. "Well, OK, What do you want to know?"

"Well, for starters, just describe for me what it was like to be raising four little kids while dad worked those endless hours in those early days. It seemed like he was hardly ever home and when he was, he was always on-call...which meant that you were on your own a lot. What was that like for you?" (Mom and Dad had four kids in five years...)

She didn't hesitate for even a moment. "Those days when I was raising my babies were the best days of my life," she said with a wistful, faraway softness in her voice. "Yes, it was tiring, but there was never a day or even a minute when I wasn't completely thankful for the privilege of being able to stay at home with the 'kinder' (Yiddish for children)."

Mom and her four "kittens" in 1957 (L-R):
Joyce, Daniel, David and Suzy.

Her response was not unexpected. She had lived through some challenging times in her life—the divorce of her parents when she was still a toddler, the lean years of the depression and then the war, and working as a secretary in the early years of her marriage to help put my father through medical school—and food on the table. (Dad also worked odd jobs during that time—driving a taxi or helping out at his father's kosher butcher shop.)

"I never wanted to do anything else," she continued. "For years I thought that life's greatest luxury was being able to stay home and raise a family. It's all I ever dreamed about. Nothing could ever come close to the sheer joy of raising my babies." These were the truest words of her heart.

Mom with Suzy, Daniel, David and Joyce in the mid-1960s in Brown County State Park in Nashville, Indiana.

Childhood memories. Lots of them came flooding back at her words. Her joy was evident in those memories. Every last one of them.

...A bitterly cold winter's day, warmly tucked in an oversized buggy with my older sister and two younger brothers, as mom — who didn't drive a car in those days—trudged her way through a blinding snowstorm to bring my older sister to her kindergarten class.

...Balmy, endless summer nights spent catching fireflies and bringing them triumphantly to Mom who sat on the porch with a grass-filled glass jar (and a properly vented metal lid) as she chatted into the night with our neighbors.

...Mom setting hot food on the table— bowls of soup, warm grilled cheese, etc. —as we came home from elementary school every day for lunch.

... Mom never taking her eyes off of my two little brothers for even a moment as they fished off the pier in the Marquette Park Lagoon on lazy summer afternoons.

...In the car with Mom 5 or 6 days a week at she ferried us to and from the synagogue for Hebrew School, Sunday School, or Sabbath services.

...Listening to her tell my brothers her fascinating tales of "Chester," his grandpa, and their housekeeper Addie—characters and stories she extemporaneously narrated for them each evening at bedtime. (We always wanted her to write down her stories. They were far better than any storybook any of us had ever read as kids.)

...Propped up with blankets and pillows in front of the TV, then hearing the sound of Mom's approaching footsteps as she came into the family room with baby aspirin, warm toast, jelly, and tea when we were sick at home. As she checked for fever, she placed a gentle hand first on our foreheads and then along the sides of our cheeks. It was the sweetest touch imaginable.

...The smell of freshly made chicken soup filling the entire house every Friday afternoon as we returned home from school.

*Mom and Dad with David, Joyce and Daniel
in the mid-1960s in Brown County State Park
in Nashville, Indiana.*

I can never recall a time when Mom wasn't home or available to us. It was my greatest comfort as a child. Many would say that she gave her whole life over to us when she could have more fully developed her own considerable talents as an artist. (She was a "Juried Artist" and my home today is filled with more than three dozen of her paintings. Visitors to our home frequently stand mesmerized by the brilliant works that adorn the walls. Yes, she's THAT good...)

But Mom would argue that she fully accomplished her life's work. She found her "passion" (as today's psychologists suggest we all do) simply by listening to the longings of her heart. She saw the rewards of her life's endeavors in the kind of people her children have become in the world—hard-working, contributing members of their communities—and parents themselves. My sister Suzy was a highly accomplished artist herself with her own thriving business; my brother Daniel is a Chiropractor and frequently published book author; my brother David, is an amazingly successful, multi-faceted businessman and entrepreneur; and I work in marketing and communications, having owned and operated my own agency for 16 years following a career in television and radio.

While I carved a career outside of the home—seeking my own "passion" as it were—parenting was a passion for me as well. But the times in which I grew up told me that I could do and have it all. (Looking back, I'm not so sure that's altogether true.) But in the end, I found myself mothering my own two children mostly guided by the memories of how loved, wanted, and cared for my Mom made me feel as a child.

Dad and I have had a lot of fun writing our book of short stories. It was Dad who suggested that I talk with Mom about her take on things during those early days of his career and raising a young family together during those tough, but in many ways "simpler" days. He knew she'd have some important things to say. Boy, did she ever.   —Joyce Kamen

The family in 2011. (Back L-R): Joyce, David, Suzy and Daniel

(Seated front): Mom & Dad.

Dad's Patients Speak

Marguerite and Marian Hall plus all our physician friends have filled me in on your great Medical genius.

Dear Dr Kamen,

Many thanks for your generosity concerning our bill with you for Paul's back. We really appreciate your kindness in forgiving this debt. We would love to have you come & visit us sometime at Liberty Bible Church in Chesterton.

We sincerely appreciate the kindness you have shown to our family. We are also grateful for the checks you returned to the family.

May God bless you for your kindness.

Dr. Kamin,

Thank you for everything you have done and what your still doing.

Ed & I don't know anyone that cared so much.

J - is for jolly.
A - is for active.
C - is for concerned.
K - is for knowledgeable.

K - is for knight in shinning armor.
A - is for acclaimed.
M - is for medical wizard
E - is for energetic
N - is for <u>numero uno</u>!

I am humbly grateful for your services and for accepting the amount we could pay, without which it wouldn't have been possible for him to have been comfortable.

Most grateful to you that I can enjoy the Holidays at home.

A Legacy of Excellence

Dad receiving the Blessed Mary Katherine Kasper Health Care Award in 1979—the highest honor bestowed by Ancilla Domini Health Services, Inc. He is shown here with Paul Kaiser, Administrator.

One More Thing...

A pratfall is funny. Usually, if done by a clown who is skilled in his trade, the faller is unhurt.

A person slipping on a banana peel is funny. It is funny to the observer but may be quite harmful to the one who slips. The faller cannot anticipate the fall and the damage to life and limb can be substantial: but to the observer, it is funny.

So the patients and medical personnel whose vignettes you have just read are funny. Some hilariously so. But at a price. Some have now departed, taken by death. Others, still among us, can recall these episodes. They also, mostly, laugh at them; in others some hurts remain.

But such is life: All human life. If you have enjoyed this book, all the better. They shall not have been hurt in vain.

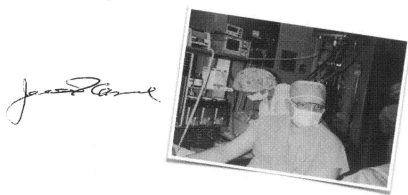

Made in the USA
Lexington, KY
15 August 2018